debbie bliss

STEP-BY-STEP
KNITTING
WORKBOOK

debbie bliss

STEP-BY-STEP
KNITTING
WORKBOOK

All the techniques and guidance you need to knit successfully, including over 20 projects

EBURY PRESS
LONDON

First published in Great Britain in 2001
5 7 9 10 8 6 4
Text and knitwear designs © Debbie Bliss, 2001
Photographs © Sandra Lane, 2001

First published by Ebury Press, Random House,
20 Vauxhall Bridge Road, London SW1V 2SA

Random House Australia (Pty) Limited
20 Alfred Street, Milsons Point, Sydney, New South Wales 2061, Australia

Random House New Zealand Limited
18 Poland Road, Glenfield, Auckland 10, New Zealand

Random House South Africa (Pty) Limited
Endulini, 5A Jubilee Road, Parktown 2193, South Africa

The Random House Group Limited Reg. No. 954009

www.randomhouse.co.uk

A CIP catalogue record for this book is available from the British Library.

Editor: Sally Harding
Designer: Christine Wood
Photographer: Sandra Lane
Stylist: Sammie Bell
Illustrations: Kate Simunek
Charts and diagrams: Antony Duke

ISBN 0 09 187873 X

Papers used by Ebury Press are natural, recyclable products made from wood grown in sustainable forests.

Colour separation by Colorlito in Milan
Printed and bound in Singapore by Tien Wah Press

contents

Introduction 6

Yarns 8
Types of yarns and care of garments 10

Knitting Basics 12
Beginning to knit 14
Knit and purl and first textures 16
Simple shaping and casting off 18
Knitting patterns 20
Abbreviations 21

Simple Shapes 22
Basics for seams and picking up stitches 24
Simple shaping class 26
◆ Baby's Cashmere Scarf and Beanie Hat 28
◆ Child's V-Neck Tunic 30
◆ Baby's Top with Moss Stitch Trim 32
◆ Raglan Sweater with Funnel Neck 34

Knitted Textures 38
Knitted textures basics 40
Cable panels class 42
Texture detailing class 44
◆ Moss Stitch Jacket 46
◆ Cable Cushion 50
◆ Aran Throw 51
◆ Child's Guernsey with Hood 54
◆ Cabled Sweater 58
◆ Man's Denim Guernsey 62

Colour Knitting 66
Colour knitting basics 68
Stranding and weaving-in class 70
Intarsia class 72
◆ Fairisle Socks 74
◆ Child's Fairisle Sweater 76
◆ Floral Cardigan with Picot Edge 80

Embroidery on Knitting 84
Embroidery basics 86
Embroidery class 88
◆ Child's Smock 90
◆ Embroidered Denim Jacket 94
◆ Embroidered Bag 100

Edgings on Knitting 102
Edgings basics 104
Edgings class 106
◆ Cashmere Baby Blanket 108
◆ Girl's Lace-Edged Cardigan 110

Buttons and Beads 114
Beads basics 116
Buttons and beads class 118
◆ Beaded Cardigan 120
◆ Beaded Moccasins 124

Yarn Information & Stockists 126
Acknowledgements 127
Index 128

Introduction

The Debbie Bliss *Knitting Workbook* is a practical guide to successful knitting, and will also, I hope, help you to create your own original handknits.

There are step-by-step diagrams to take you through the basics and to help you produce more professional garments, and beautiful photographs of objects that have inspired me in my own designs and may help you source your own ideas.

There are over 20 projects to knit, from the very simple like the baby's cashmere garter stitch scarf to the more advanced floral cardigan or Aran throw. Each design will help you to practice and perfect your knitting techniques.

My *Knitting Workbook* is aimed at both new knitters who can gain confidence as they tackle the simpler projects and the more experienced knitters who want to refresh or improve their techniques and begin to create their own ideas.

I have loved the opportunity not only to design the projects here but also to share my creative and design inspiration.

Yarns From rustic
tweeds to sensuous silks – choose
a yarn to suit the look and mood

Types of yarns

Fibres are divided into two main categories, natural and synthetic. Natural fibres are then divided into animal fibres – wool, angora, cashmere, silk, etc. – and those from vegetable fibres, such as cotton, linen and hemp. My preference is to use, where possible, natural fibres or those with a small amount of man-made fibres.

WOOL

Wool, spun from the fleece of sheep, is the yarn that is the most commonly associated with knitting. It has many excellent properties as it is durable, elastic and warm in the winter.

Wool yarn is particularly good for working colour patterns since the fibres adhere together and help prevent Fair Isle or intarsia patterns from 'pulling away' and forming gaps.

Some knitters also find that simple stitch patterns such as garter stitch and moss stitch can look neater, the knitted fabric more even, in a wool rather than a cotton yarn.

COTTON

Cotton yarn, made from a natural plant fibre, is warm in the winter and cool in the summer, making it an ideal all-seasons fibre. I prefer to work in cotton, since I find that the resulting knitted garments have a special crispness and that the stitch detailing really stands out.

On the down side, I always make sure that I use a really good-quality cotton as the knitted cotton fabric, if it has been worked in a poorer quality cotton, can droop and loose its elasticity after washing, particularly on ribbed borders.

COTTON AND WOOL YARN

Knitting yarn that is made of a blend of cotton and wool fibres is particularly good for children's knitwear. This is because the wool content gives elasticity for comfort and the cotton content is perfect for those children who find wool fibres scratchy and irritating on the skin.

CASHMERE

Made from the underhair of a particular Asian goat, cashmere yarn will always be associated with the ultimate in luxury. It is absolutely beautiful and unbelievably soft to the touch. It is also extremely expensive due to the shortage of supply. If you find the cost prohibitive, try it for small scarves or baby items.

DENIM YARN

Denim yarn is one of my all time favourites. Garments knitted in denim yarn actually improve with age! As it is washed and worn the fabric fades just like your jeans, highlighting stitch patterns. An added bonus – as it is machine washable and can be tumble dried, it is ideal for busy mums with grubby kids.

ALPACA

Often as soft as cashmere, alpaca yarn is a cheaper alternative. Made from an animal related to the llama, it is similar to, but less hairy than, mohair.

LINEN

Made from the flax plant, linen yarn is one of the earliest fibres used by man in textiles. It is beautiful in classic simple shapes, but can be rather hard to the touch.

SILK YARN

Silk is a fibre produced by certain caterpillars as the spin their cocoon. Its beauty can make up for some of its less practical properties, for it can be inclined to pill and is not a very elastic yarn.

BUYING YARN FOR A KNITTING PATTERN

Try to buy the yarn specified in your knitting pattern; however, if you prefer to use a substitute, buy a yarn that is the same weight and has the same tension (see Tension on page 20), and where possible the same fibre content. If you use a synthetic yarn instead of a natural fibre, or even wool where cotton had been originally used, the stitch patterns may appear softer and less delineated. Synthetics can also appear limp, which means that the crispness of the original garment will have been lost. It is essential to check metreage or yardage. Yarn that weighs the same may have different lengths, and you may need to buy more or less yarn.

Check the ball band on the yarn. Most yarn labels now carry all the information you need about fibre content, washing instructions, weight and metreage or yardage. Some of them will tell you the knitting needle sizes to use and the standard tension (or stitch size) these create.

It is essential to check the dye lot number on the yarn label. Yarns are dyed in batches or lots which can sometimes vary quite considerably. Your retailer may not have the same dye lot later on, so try and buy all your yarn for a project at the same time. If you know that sometimes you require extra yarn to that quoted in a pattern, buy more. If it is not possible to buy the amount you need all in one dye lot, work the borders on the lower edges or the neckband in the odd one, since the colour change is less likely to show here.

Care of garments

Taking care of your knitted garments is important. If you have invested all that time and labour into knitting them, you want them to look good for as long as possible. Follow these simple care guidelines for the best results.

WASHING AND DRYING YOUR KNITTING

Check the ball band on your yarn for washing instructions. Many yarns can now be machine washed on a delicate wool cycle. You may find it helpful to make a note of the measurements of the garment, such as the width and length, prior to washing. After washing, lay the garment flat and check the measurements again to see if they are the same. If not, smooth and pat it back into shape.

Natural fibres are usually best hand washed, even if the ball band says otherwise. I find that after successive machine washes, cotton in particular can become rather hard. Use soap flakes specially created for hand knits, and warm rather than hot water. Handle the knits gently in the water – do not rub or wring because this can felt the fabric. Rinse well to get rid of any soap, and squeeze out excess water. You may need to get rid of more water by rolling the garment in a towel, or you can use the delicate spin cycle of the washing machine. Dry the garment by laying it out flat on top of a towel to absorb moisture, smooth and pat into shape. Do not dry knits near direct heat such as a radiator.

Store your knits loosely folded to allow the air to circulate.

DENIM YARN CARE

Rowan *Denim* yarn will shrink and fade when it is washed. It is dyed with real indigo dye which only coats the surface of the yarn, so it has a white core that is gradually exposed during washing and wearing. When washed for the first time, the yarn will shrink by up to a fifth in length, but not width. All the necessary adjustments will have been made in the knitting pattern instructions that call for this denim yarn.

The knitted pieces should be washed separately at a water temperature of 60–70° C (140–158° F) along with a small ball of yarn for seams. The pieces can then be tumble dried or dried flat, as explained in full on the yarn label, before you sew up the garment.

Knitting Basics

Cast on, cast off, knit one, purl one – four easy
steps to simple knitwear

Beginning to knit

The first step when beginning to knit is to cast on. There are several ways of doing this, but there are two cast ons – the thumb and the cable methods – that seem to be the most frequently used. The best one to choose is the one that you feel most comfortable with, or that produces the kind of edge you prefer. You may choose to use a different cast-on technique depending on where it occurs on the garment. The cable cast on, for example, produces a firm edge that can be useful in an area that may get a lot of wear, such as on sleeve cuffs.

Starting with a slip knot

To start most cast-on methods, you first need to make a simple slip knot, also called a 'slip loop'. This makes the slip knot the very first 'stitch' that you cast on your knitting needle. To make it clear which end of the yarn comes from the yarn ball, the loose end is shown short so it fits in the diagram – but in reality you should leave a long loose end so it can either be darned in or used to sew the seam.

1 Wind the yarn twice around fingers on your left hand to make a circle of yarn as shown in the inset. With the knitting needle, pull a loop of the yarn attached to the ball through the yarn circle on your fingers.

2 Then pull both ends of the yarn to tighten the slip knot on the knitting needle. You are now ready to use one of the following cast-on methods to cast stitches onto your knitting needle.

Thumb cast on (English)

I use the thumb cast on, because as a fairly tight knitter I find it gives me a fast, fluid cast on with an edge that I like. It has quite a bit of 'give' in it, which makes it ideal for edges that need some flexibility and stretch, for instance on the roll-up brim of a beanie hat (see Beanie Hat on page 28).

One word of warning, however – because you are casting on and working towards the end of the yarn (unlike two-needle methods where you work towards the ball), you have to predict how much yarn is needed for the amount of stitches required. You may find that you are left with a few more stitches to make and not enough yarn to make them with. Depending on the thickness of the yarn, one metre (39 inches) creates about 100 stitches. However, if you are unsure, over-compensate by allowing more yarn than you think you need. You can always use the extra length to sew up the seams.

Generally, knitters are taught to use a slip knot to begin with when casting on with this method, but once you become confident with the technique, rather than use a slip knot, work the first stitch by simply laying the yarn over your thumb from front to back and holding the yarn as before with the yarn over the right needle – then knit into the thumb loop. I find that this gives a slightly neater edge.

1 Make a slip knot as shown above, leaving a long tail. With the slip knot on the needle in your right hand and the yarn that comes from the ball over your index finger, wrap the tail end of the yarn over your left thumb from front to back, securing the yarn in your palm with your fingers.

2 Then insert the knitting needle upwards through the yarn loop on your left thumb.

3 Next, with the right index finger, wrap the yarn from the ball up and over the point of the knitting needle.

4 Then draw the yarn through the loop on your thumb to form a new stitch on the knitting needle. Lastly, let the yarn loop slip off your left thumb and pull the loose end to tighten up the stitch. Repeat these steps to make the stitches you need.

Thumb cast on (Continental)

This cast on is worked in the same way as the English thumb cast on, except that both ends of the yarn are held in the left hand. Because knitters on the continent usually knit with the working yarn held in their left hand, they generally prefer this type of thumb cast on over the 'English' method. As explained on the previous page, you can do without the slip knot if you prefer.

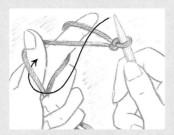

1 Hold the needle with the slip knot in your right hand and the tail end of the yarn in your left hand as for the English method, but put the yarn from the ball over the left index finger and secure both ends in your palm with your fingers. To begin, insert the knitting needle through the thumb loop as shown by the arrow.

2 Then 'grab' the yarn on the index finger with the knitting needle as shown by the arrow, and pull a loop through the loop on the thumb.

3 Let the yarn loop slip off your left thumb and pull both ends to tighten up the new cast-on stitch. Continue casting on in this way until you have the stitches you need.

CAST-ON TIP

On reversible fabrics, after casting on you can decide which is the wrong side of the fabric. You can then check this by noticing whether the 'tail' of your cast-on yarn is on the left- or right-hand side of the work. With the thumb cast on, this tail will be at the opposite end of the work to the cable cast on. (Although your fabric is reversible, you will need to know which is the right side and which the wrong side when working shaping, etc.)

Cable cast on

The cable cast on is a popular method of casting on that creates a firm edge. It can be a good cast onto use where an elastic, but sturdier, foundation row would be an advantage. Those with a standard to tight 'tension' like myself may find it more difficult to insert the knitting needle between the stitches and pull the yarn through, so make sure that you do not tighten up each new stitch on the left-hand needle too much. (See more about your knitting tension on page 20.)

1 Make a slip knot as shown on the previous page. Then hold the knitting needle with the slip knot in your left hand and insert the right-hand needle from left to right and from front to back through the slip knot. Wrap the yarn from the ball up and over the point of the right-hand needle as shown.

2 With the right-hand needle, draw a loop through the slip knot to make a new stitch. Do not drop the stitch from the left-hand needle, but instead slip the new stitch onto the left-hand needle as shown.

3 Then insert the right-hand needle between the two stitches on the left-hand needle and wrap the yarn around the point of the right-hand needle.

4 Pull the yarn through to make a new stitch. and then place the new stitch on left-hand needle as before. Repeat the last two steps to make the stitches you need.

Knit and purl

After casting on stitches, you knit or purl them according to what your knitting patterns requires. Though the basic techniques for making knit or purl stitches are very simple, they are what builds up the whole knitted fabric.

The knit stitch

The knit stitch is the very first stitch you will learn and forms a reversible fabric called garter stitch. Follow the three steps below to make the knit stitch. When you have worked all the stitches from the left-hand needle onto the right-hand needle you have completed a 'row'. You then turn the work, transferring the needle with all the stitches to the left-hand, and continue as before.

1 With the cast-on stitches on the needle in your left hand, insert the right-hand needle from left to right and from front to back through first cast-on stitch.

2 Then take the yarn from the ball on your index finger (the working yarn) around the point of the right-hand needle.

3 Draw the right-hand needle and yarn through the stitch, thus forming a new stitch on the right-hand needle, and at the same time slip the original stitch off the left-hand needle. Repeat these steps until all the stitches from the left-hand needle have been worked. This is called a row.

The purl stitch

After the knit stitch, the next stitch to discover is the purl stitch. This stitch is the reverse of the knit stitch, but if every row is worked as a purl row it creates the same fabric as if you had knitted every row – garter stitch. If you alternate purl rows with knit rows, you create the most commonly used knitted fabric, stocking stitch. When working stocking stitch try to keep your tension consistent on both your knit and purl rows. Uneven fabric can be produced by working one side tighter or looser than the other, giving a 'stripey' effect.

1 With the yarn to the front of the work, insert the right-hand needle from right to left into the front of the first stitch on the left-hand needle.

2 Then take the yarn from the ball on your index finger (the working yarn) around the point of the right-hand needle.

3 Draw the right-hand needle and the yarn through the stitch, thus forming a new stitch on the right-hand needle, and at the same time slip the original stitch off the left-hand needle. Repeat these steps until all the stitches have been worked.

First textures

By combining knit and purl stitches in various ways many different knitted textures can be created. The most basic textures and the ones used the most frequently are garter stitch, stocking stitch, reverse stocking stitch, ribbing and moss stitch.

Garter stitch

Ideal for beginners, garter stitch is the simplest of them all. However, care should be taken with it as it can show up inconsistencies in your knitting. Garter stitch is seen at its best when worked in a natural fibre, particularly pure wool, and over fairly small areas, such as in a baby garment (see the Baby's Cashmere Scarf and Beanie Hat on page 29). It makes a good detail used on collars and edgings. However, it can take a little longer to knit up than stocking stitch because two rows of garter stitch only show as one.

Stitch pattern for garter stitch
Cast on any number of stitches.
Knit every row.

Double ribbing

Ribbings are usually worked as lower borders or neckbands on garments. By pulling the fabric in, ribs prevent garments from fluting at the lower edge and ensure that cuffs fit snugly around the wrist. My own favourite is the '2 by 2' or 'double' rib – it is simple, but I feel is more distinctive than the single rib.

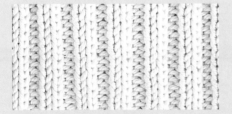

Stitch pattern for double rib
Cast on a multiple of 4 stitches, plus 2 extra.
1st row K2, *p2, k2; repeat from * to end.
2nd row P2, *k2, p2; repeat from * to end.
Repeat the 1st and 2nd rows to form double rib.

Stocking stitch

Stocking stitch is the basis of most knitwear and can be used to create the simplest of garments. It makes an excellent background to show shaping details or embellishments. The knit rows on stocking stitch are considered to be the right side of the fabric and the purl rows, the wrong side.

Stitch pattern for stocking stitch
Cast on any number of stitches.
1st row (right side) Knit.
2nd row (wrong side) Purl.
Repeat the 1st and 2nd rows to form stocking stitch.

Moss (seed) stitch

Moss stitch is my favourite of all of the simple stitch patterns. It is perfect not only worked as an allover pattern on a garment (see the Moss Stitch Jacket on page 47), but also as detailing on collars, lower borders and front bands it makes a beautiful alternative to ribbing. Moss stitch does not knit up as quickly as some patterns because the yarn is being constantly carried back and forth between the front and the back of the work.

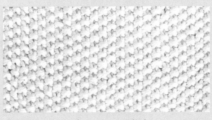

Stitch pattern for moss stitch
Cast on an uneven number of stitches.
1st row K1, *p1, k1; repeat from * to end.
Repeat this row to form moss stitch.

Reverse stocking stitch

Reverse stocking stitch fabric is the reverse side of stocking stitch. It is usually used as a background on which cables are worked, as it makes the stocking stitch cables stand out more clearly. I prefer to see it only used in small areas since it can make the fabric look rather bare and uninteresting.

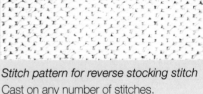

Stitch pattern for reverse stocking stitch
Cast on any number of stitches.
1st row (right side) Purl.
2nd row (wrong side) Knit.
Repeat the 1st and 2nd rows to form reverse stocking stitch.

Double moss stitch

Based on single moss stitch, double moss stitch is worked over double the amount of stitches and rows. This creates a more textured, raised effect which works particularly well as a selvedge on Aran designs.

Stitch pattern for double moss stitch
Cast on a multiple of 4 stitches, plus 2 extra.
1st row K2, *p2, k2; repeat from * to end.
2nd row P2, *k2, p2; repeat from * to end.
3rd row P2, *k2, p2; repeat from * to end.
4th row K2, *p2, k2; repeat from * to end.
Repeat 1st to 4th rows to form moss stitch.

Simple shaping and casting off

To shape your knitting – for example along armhole, neck and sleeve edges – there are various techniques for increasing or decreasing the number of stitches on your needle. The simplest, most frequently used increases and decreases are given on these two pages along with how to 'cast off' or end your knitting.

Increases

Increases are worked to make your knitted fabric wider by adding to the number of stitches. They are most often used when shaping sleeves or after completing ribbing on the lower edges of backs, fronts and sleeves.

Inceases can be used decoratively to add detailing to an otherwise plain design (see the Raglan Sweater on page 34). Decorative increases like this are placed two or three stitches from the edge of the knitting so that they can be seen after the garment has been sewn up.

Increasing when working stocking stitch is relatively simple, but when working more complex stitch patterns, check to see if your instructions tell you to work extra increased stitches into the pattern.

Yarn over increases are usually worked in lace patterns, followed by a decrease to create a hole or eyelet.

INCREASE ONE ('inc one')

1 Insert the the right-hand needle into the front of the next stitch, then knit the stitch but leave it on the left-hand needle.

2 Insert the right-hand needle into the back of the same stitch and knit it. Then slip the original stitch off the needle. You now have an extra stitch on the right-hand needle.

MAKE ONE ('m1')

 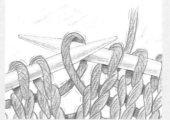

1 Insert the left-hand needle from front to back under the horizontal strand between the stitch just worked on the right-hand needle and the first stitch on the left-hand needle.

2 Knit into the back of the loop to twist it, thus preventing a hole. Then drop the strand from the left-hand needle. This forms a new stitch on the right-hand needle.

YARN OVER BETWEEN KNIT STITCHES ('yf')

Bring the yarn forward between the two needles, from the back to the front of the work. Taking the yarn over the needle to do so, knit the next stitch.

YARN OVER BETWEEN A KNIT AND A PURL ('yrn')

Bring the yarn forward between the two needles from the back to the front of the work, and take it over the top of the needle to the back again and then forward between the needles. Then purl the next stitch.

YARN OVER BETWEEN PURL STITCHES ('yrn')

Bring the yarn over the needle to the back, then between the two needles to the front. Then purl the next stitch.

YARN OVER BETWEEN A PURL AND A KNIT ('yon')

Take the yarn from the front over the needle to the back. Then knit the next stitch.

Decreases

Decreases are used to make your fabric narrower by reducing the number of stitches. They are most often used when shaping necklines or the tops of sleeves. As with increases, decreases can form decorative detailing a few stitches from the edge, where different techniques are used to make the decreases slant to the right or left. This type of shaping, called 'fully fashioned', can be useful when shaping necks. By working 'knit 2 together' on the right neck edge and 'slip 1, knit 1, pass slipped stitch over' on the left side a neater edge is created, making it is easier to pick up stitches around the neck for the neckband or collar. Worked two stitches in from the neckline edge, the slanting stitches can provide an interesting detail around the neck (see Child's Tunic on page 31).

KNIT 2 TOGETHER
('k2tog' or 'dec one')

On a knit row, insert the right-hand needle from left to right through the next two stitches on the left-hand needle and knit them together. One stitch has been decreased.

PURL 2 TOGETHER
('p2tog' or 'dec one')

On a purl row, insert the right-hand needle from right to left through next two stitches on the left-hand needle. Then purl them together. One stitch has been decreased.

SLIP 1, KNIT 1, PASS SLIPPED STITCH OVER ('psso')

1 Insert the right-hand needle into the next stitch on the left-hand needle and slip it onto the right-hand needle without knitting it. Knit the next stitch. Then insert the left-hand needle into the slipped stitch as shown.

2 With the left-hand needle, lift the slipped stitch over the knitted stitch as shown and off the right-hand needle.

Casting off

Casting off is the method used after you have completed your knitting to secure the stitches so they do not unravel. It is important that the cast-off edge is neither too tight nor too loose, and that it is elastic. This is particularly important when casting off on a neckband so that it can be pulled easily over the head. Casting off is also used to make most types of buttonholes and when more than one stitch needs to be decreased at once. Unless otherwise stated, cast off in the stitch pattern being used on the garment.

KNIT CAST OFF

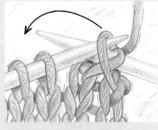

1 Knit two stitches. Then insert the left-hand needle into the first stitch knitted on the right-hand needle and lift this stitch over the second stitch and off the right-hand needle.

2 One stitch is now on the right-hand needle. Knit the next stitch. Repeat the first step until all the stitches have been cast off. Then pull the yarn through the last stitch to fasten off.

PURL CAST OFF

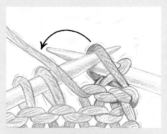

1 Purl two stitches. Insert the left-hand needle into the back of the first stitch worked on the right-hand needle and lift this stitch over the second stitch and off the right-hand needle.

2 One stitch is now on the right-hand needle. Purl the next stitch. Repeat the first step untill all the stitches have been cast off. Then pull the yarn through the last stitch to fasten off.

Knitting patterns

Most patterns adhere to a fairly recognizable structure. They will tell you what yarn to use, how much of it to buy, and needle sizes, measurements, tension and abbreviations. First of all, check that the pattern suits your capabilities. If you are a beginner, choose a design that is fairly simple or you may be disheartened to find yourself struggling with techniques and stitch patterns that you are not quite ready to tackle.

Reading instructions

I used to tell knitters to read the pattern carefully first, but I am changing my views on this as I feel that some parts of the pattern, which are simple and make sense when you are actually knitting them, seem confusing when reading through initially. Some instructions only really make sense when the knitting is on the knitting needles.

But do read the materials list before you leave the shop with your pattern and yarn. Check the equipment you need carefully. There is nothing worse than getting home eager to start your project, only to find that you assumed that a certain weight of yarn required the most obvious needle size and that for that particular pattern you need needles you do not have, or that a cable needle was required. Check, too, for additional materials that you may need, such as a zipper, etc. Buttons are sometimes best left to be chosen after the garment has been finished to get a sense of size and the most appropriate design.

Also, look at the measurements on the knitting instructions before buying yarn, to be sure what size you want to knit. Most patterns now quote the actual finished knitted size of the garment rather than just the bust/chest measurements of the wearer. The actual measurements will tell you the width around the whole garment and this will tell you how much ease a garment has, whether it is a generous, baggy style or slim fitting. If you wish to make up the design with less or more ease, you may just need to knit the size smaller or larger size quoted. If you are unsure, measure an existing garment you have, to compare. The length of the garment is usually taken from the shoulder shaping to the cast-on edge

Following pattern instructions

Most patterns – depending on the style – are written for a range of sizes. The smallest size is given first in the instructions and appears outside of the round () brackets (or parentheses); the larger sizes are given inside the brackets. Make sure, as you follow the pattern, that you are consistently using the right stitches for your size – it is only too easy to switch sizes inside the brackets. One way to avoid this is to go through the instructions first and mark the size you are knitting with a coloured pen or highlighter.

Work instructions given in square [ ] brackets the number of times stated afterwards. Where 0 appears, no stitches or rows are worked for this size.

There is rarely space in a knitting pattern to write out all the instructions in full. For this reason, abbreviations are sometimes used throughout the pattern, but explained in full before the pattern starts – or, in a book, on a page dedicated to abbreviations.

Yarn for your knitting pattern

Where possible use the yarn that has been quoted in the pattern. This yarn will have been tried and tested in the sample garment, and the designer will have worked with it because it produces the best possible look for the design. (For more about buying yarn for your knitting, see page 10).

Tension

It is crucial to check your tension before you embark on any project. 'Tension' is the number of stitches and rows to a centimetre (inch) and is also known as 'stitch gauge' or simply 'gauge'. The tension determines the measurements of a garment, so it is very important that you obtain the same number of rows and stitches as the designer.

A small difference over 10 centimetres (4 inches) can add up to a considerable amount over the complete width of the knitted garment. If your tension is looser or tighter than the one stated in the knitting pattern, your garment will be larger or smaller than the original garment. So taking time out for 15 minutes to work a tension square before you start can save a lot of disappointment later on.

The size of the stitch depends on the yarn, the size of the knitting needles and your control of the yarn. It can also depend on mood – many knitters will have experienced a tighter tension when stress levels are higher!

Using the same yarn and needles and stitch pattern that the tension has been measured over in the pattern, knit a sample at least 13 centimetres (5½ inches) square. Then smooth out the square on a flat surface.

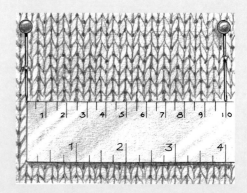

To check stitch tension, place a ruler (a cloth tape meaure can be less accurate) horizontally on the fabric and mark 10 centimetres (4 inches) with pins. Count the number of stitches

between the pins. To check row tension, place a ruler vertically, mark 10 centimetres (4 inches) with pins and count the number of rows. If the number of stitches and rows is greater than it says in the pattern, your tension is tighter. This can usually be regulated by using larger needles. If the number of stitches is fewer than the specified number, your tension is looser and you should change to smaller needles. Your tension may change from that of your sample when knitting the actual garment, as your knitting can alter when working across more stitches.

Needle conversion chart

This needle coversion chart covers all the knitting needle sizes used for the patterns in this book.

Metric	UK sizes	US sizes
2¾mm	No 12	size 2
3mm	No 11	size 3
3¼mm	No 10	size 3
3¾mm	No 9	size 5
4mm	No 8	size 6
4½mm	No 7	size 7

UK and US knitting terminology

The following terms that are used in the book may be unfamiliar to US readers.

UK term	US term
Aran wool	'fisherman' yarn
ball band	yarn wrapper or label
brackets, round	parentheses
brackets, square	brackets
cast off	bind off
DK (double knitting)	a yarn weight between sport and worsted
double moss stitch	double seed stitch
every alternate row	every other row
make up	finish
moss stitch	seed stitch
stocking stitch	stockinette stitch
tension	gauge
welt	lower borders on sweater front and back
yf	yarn over (yo), or yarn to front of work between two needles
yon, yrn	yarn over (yo)

Abbreviations

A few knitting terms may be unfamiliar to some readers. The list below explains the abbreviations used in this book. If a knitting pattern has more specific abbreviations, they appear at the beginning of the pattern.

alt = alternate
beg = begin(ning)
cont = continu(e)(ing)
cm = centimetre(s)
dec = decrease(e)(ing)
foll = follow(ing)
g = gram(mes)
in = inch(es)
inc = increas(e)(ing)
inc one = increase one st by working into the front and back of the stitch
k = knit
m1 = make one by picking up the loop lying between the stitch just worked and next stitch and working into the back of it
mm = millimetre(s)
oz = ounce(s)
patt = pattern
p = purl
psso = pass slipped stitch over
rem = remain(ing)
rep = repeat(ing)
RS = right side
skpo = slip one, knit one, pass slipped stitch over
sl = slip
st(s) = stitch(es)
st st = stocking stitch
tbl = through back of loop(s)
tog = together
WS = wrong side
yb = yarn back
yf = yarn forward
yon = yarn over needle
yrn = yarn around needle

Simple Shapes

Simplicity can be the key to perfection – whether in the natural world or in pared-down design

Basics for seams and picking up stitches

The making up of a garment and adding picked up borders is the last, but one of the most important, stages in producing a professional garment. A beautifully knitted garment can be ruined by careless sewing up, or unevenly picked up borders, as the knitter hurries to complete the project. Here are the basic techniques for helping you perfect those finishing touches.

Seams

The seam that I use for almost all sewing up is mattress stitch, which produces a wonderful invisible seam. It works well on any yarn, and makes a completely straight seam, as the same amount is taken up on each side – this also means that the knitted pieces should not need to be pinned together first. I find mattress stitch particularly invaluable when sewing seams on Fair Isle bands or striped pieces of knitting.

I use other types of seams less frequently, but they do have their uses. For instance, backstitch can sometimes be useful for sewing in a sleeve head, to neatly ease in the fullness. It is also good for catching in loose strands of yarn on colourwork seams, where there can be a lot of short ends along the selvedge. Just remember when using backstitch to sew up your knitting that it is important to ensure that you work in a completely straight line.

The seam for joining two cast-off edges is handy for shoulder seams, while the seam for joining a cast-off edge with a side edge (selvedge) is usually used when sewing a sleeve onto the body on a dropped shoulder style.

It is best to leave a long tail at the casting-on stage to sew up your knitting with, so that the sewing up yarn is already secured in place. If this is not possible, when first securing the thread for the seam, you should leave a length that can be darned in afterwards. All seams on knitting should be sewn with a large blunt-ended yarn or tapestry needle to avoid splitting the yarn.

BEGINNING A SEAM

With the right sides of the knitting facing you and using the long tail left from your cast-on row, thread the strand into your blunt-ended sewing needle. Insert the sewing needle from back to front through the corner stitch of the other piece of knitting. Then make a figure of eight, and insert the needle from back to front into the stitch with the long tail. Pull the thread through to close the gap between the two pieces of knitting.

MATTRESS STITCH ON STOCKING STITCH

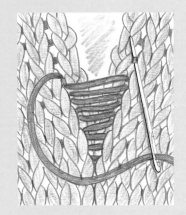

With the right sides of the knitting facing you, insert the needle under the horizontal bar between the first stitch and next stitch. Then insert the needle under the same bar on the other piece. Continue to do this, drawing up the thread to form the seam.

RIB SEAM – JOINING TWO KNIT-STITCH EDGES

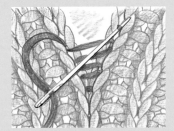

Insert the needle under a horizontal bar in the centre of a knit stitch at the edge of one piece of knitting and then at the edge of the other piece. Continue to do this, drawing up the thread to form one complete knit stitch along the seam.

RIB SEAM – JOINING TWO PURL-STITCH EDGES

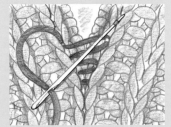

Skip the purl stitch at the edge of each piece of knitting and join the seam at the centre of knit stitches, as for joining two knit-stitch edges.

RIB SEAM – JOINING KNIT- AND PURL-STITCH EDGES

Skip the purl stitch at the edge of one piece of knitting and join the seam at the centre of knit stitches, as for joining two knit-stitch edges.

JOINING TWO CAST-OFF EDGES

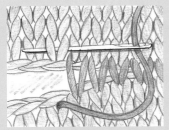 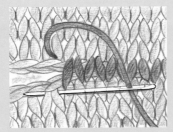

1 With the cast-off edges butted together, bring the needle out in the centre of the first stitch just below the cast-off edge on one piece. Insert the needle through the centre of the first stitch on the other piece and out through the centre of the next stitch.

2 Next, insert the needle through the centre of the first stitch on the first piece again and out through the centre of the stitch next to it. Continue in this way until the seam is completed.

JOINING A CAST-OFF EDGE AND A SELVEDGE EDGE

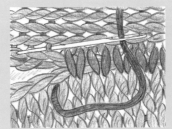

Bring the needle back to front through the centre of the first stitch on the cast-off edge. Then insert it under one or two horizontal strands between the first and second stitches on the selvedge and back through the centre of the same cast-off stitch. Continue in this way until the seam is completed.

BACKSTITCH

1 With right sides placed side by side and using the long tail of yarn from the cast-on edge, secure the seam by taking the needle twice around the outer edges from back to front. Then bring the needle through both thicknesses no more than 1cm (¼in) from where the yarn last came out.

2 Insert the needle back into the point where the yarn came out from the last stitch and bring the needle back through the same distance ahead of the emerging yarn. Repeat these steps, keeping stitches of uniform length and in an absolutely straight line.

Picking up stitches

'Picking up stitches' is a technique used when you need to knit a border directly onto a piece of knitting, for instance to add button bands on a cardigan or a neckband along a neck edge. To do this, you draw loops through the knitting with the tip of your knitting needle, forming stitches directly onto your needle.

Your knitting pattern will tell you how many stitches to pick up, and this should be done evenly. In the pattern, the instruction usually reads 'pick up and knit'.

ALONG A SELVEDGE

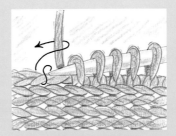

With the right side of the knitting facing, insert the knitting needle from front to back between the first and second stitches of the first row. Wrap the yarn around the needle and pull a loop through to form a new stitch on the needle. Continue in this way along the edge of the knitting.

ALONG A NECK EDGE

On a neck edge, work along the straight edges as for a selvedge. But along the curved edges, insert the needle through the centre of the stitch below the shaping (to avoid large gaps) and pull a loop of yarn through to form a new stitch on the needle.

Simple shaping class

I like to use very simple shapes in my designs. They give me the opportunity not only to concentrate on creating complex patterns in stitch and colour, but also, when using a basic stitch such as moss stitch or stocking stitch, to enhance the beautiful texture with clean lines.

Designing simple sweater shapes

When designing an Aran sweater (see Cable Panels Class on page 42) or knitwear with large colour motifs, I usually prefer to use a dropped shoulder line rather than a set-in sleeve. The flat sleeve top and the straight edge of the garment allow me to carry stitch patterns and colourwork knitting straight up the sides without them being interrupted by the decreasing required for armhole and sleeve top shaping.

Heavily textured knits in thick yarns also need the ease allowance that this simple sleeve shape gives – so that there is no bulky fabric at the armhole. This is particularly important when designing for children. They are used to wearing the soft fabric of fleeces and need to feel comfortable in knitwear. Wearing sweaters in basic shapes and with generous sizing, small children will feel as free in their handknits as in their sweatshirts and T-shirts.

If you want to create your own simple knit, measure the proportions of a basic sweatshirt shape that you have that has straight sides and dropped shoulders. Write down the length and width of the body, and the top of sleeve width, bottom of sleeve width and length. Then work a swatch in a basic stitch such as stocking stitch or moss stitch, and find out how many stitches and rows you have to 10 centimetres (4 inches). With this information, you can work out how many stitches and rows you would need for the measurements you require, and how many stitches you would need to increase on the sleeves. Look at other similar knitting patterns if you are not quite sure how to begin, or if you want to see how simple necks are created. If you feel that this would be too complicated to start with, begin with a simple cushion or bag.

Detailing simply shaped garments

Simple shapes can be enhanced by the introduction of carefully selected detailing. Fully fashioned shaping on stocking stitch, for instance, creates a subtle effect, as the stitches slant in different directions, and a garter-stitch edge and side vent on a tunic design is both practical and stylish. Delicate edgings can be used on hems as a pretty alternative to ribs. Traditional styles, such as classic Fair Isles, can be transformed by shaping at the sides to give a fitted, tailored look – this can be a welcome change sometimes from the oversized, body-obscuring knits.

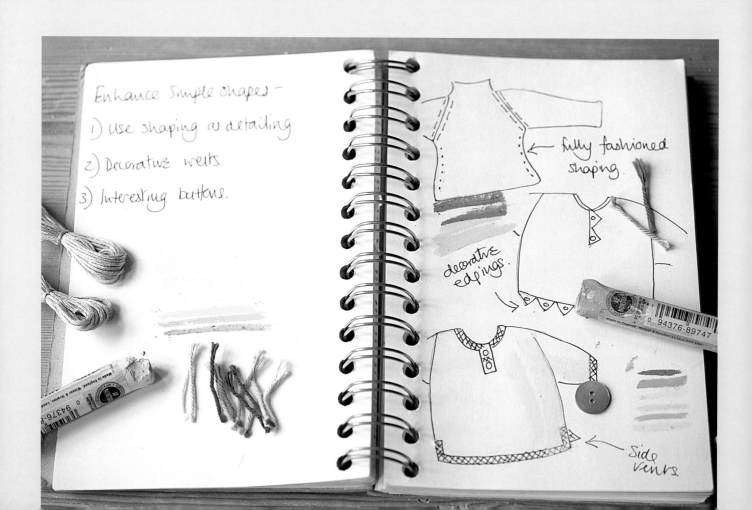

Finishing on simple shapes

The simpler the shape and the stitch pattern, the more important it is that your techniques for sewing up are of a really high standard. The seams on simple shapes will show more, and where the shaping has been used to be decorative, as in the Raglan Sweater on page 34, the seams must be as perfect as possible.

Proportions on simple shapes

You should also keep in mind that pared-down shapes emphasize proportion. As a designer, I care passionately that the design I have created has the measurements that I wanted. As I am thinking about the design, I know that I want it to be short and boxy, or long and lean. If a knitter's tension is different to the one quoted in the pattern and when completed the garment is wider or skinnier, shorter or longer, this will affect the way the design looks. A simple but stylish handknit can then begin to look very average.

Baby's Cashmere Scarf and Beanie Hat

This garter stitch scarf is perfect for beginners, and knitted in cashmere it would make an ideal luxury gift for a new baby. The beanie hat has a snug fit with a small rolled brim.

MATERIALS
For the set
3(4) x 25g (1oz) balls of Jaeger *Cashmere*
Pair of 3¹⁄₄mm (UK No 10/US size 3) knitting needles

SIZE AND MEASUREMENTS

Hat to fit ages	0–3		3–6	months
Scarf to fit ages	3–6	months		
Scarf width	12	cm		
	4³⁄₄	in		
Scarf length	63	cm		
	24³⁄₄	in		

TENSION
25 sts and 46 rows to 10cm/4in over garter st using 3¹⁄₄mm (UK No 10/US size 3) needles.

ABBREVIATIONS
See page 21.

SCARF
TO MAKE
With 3¹⁄₄mm (No 10/US 3)needles, cast on 30 sts.
Work in garter st (k every row) until scarf measures 63cm/24³⁄₄in from cast-on edge.
Cast off.

HAT
TO MAKE
With 3¹⁄₄mm (No 10/US 3)needles, cast on 91(101) sts.
Starting with a k row, work 8 rows in st st for rolled edging.
Cont in garter st (k every row) until hat measures 15(18)cm/6(7)in from cast-on edge.
Shape Top
Cont in garter st throughout, beg shaping on next row as foll:
Next row K1, [k2tog, k8] 9(10) times. 82(91) sts.
Work 3 rows without shaping.
Next row K1, [k2tog, k7] 9(10) times. 73(81) sts.
Work 3 rows without shaping.
Next row K1, [k2tog, k6] 9(10) times. 64(71) sts.
Work 3 rows without shaping.
Next row K1, [k2tog, k5] 9(10) times. 55(61) sts.
Work 3 rows without shaping.
Next row K1, [k2tog, k4] 9(10) times. 46(51) sts.

Work 1 row without shaping.
Next row K1, [k2tog, k3] 9(10) times. 37(41) sts.
Work 1 row without shaping.
Next row K1, [k2tog, k2] 9(10) times. 28(31) sts.
Work 1 row without shaping.
Next row K1, [k2tog, k1] 9(10) times. 19(21) sts.
Next row K1, [k2tog] to end. 10(11) sts.
Break off yarn, leaving a long loose end.

TO MAKE UP
Using a yarn needle, thread loose end through sts on knitting needle and drop sts from knitting needle. Pull loose end to gather sts and secure; but do not break off yarn. Then use loose end to join hat seam, reversing st st section of seam for roll back.

The thumb method of casting on is ideal for this beanie hat. It gives a more elastic foundation row for the turned-up, rolled edge.

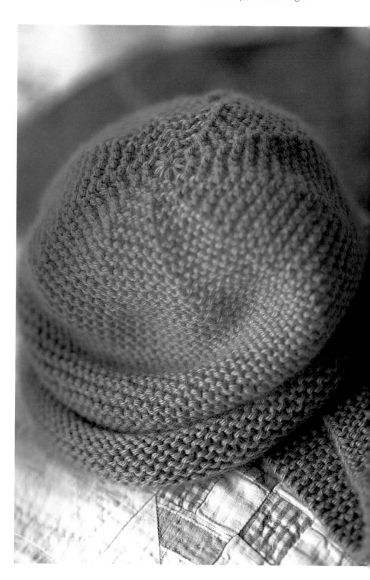

Child's V-Neck Tunic

The beauty of this garment is in the detailing. A garter stitch border and a side vent for ease of movement are combined with fully fashioned shaping around the neck.

MATERIALS

6(7:8) x 50g (1¾oz) balls Rowan *Cotton Glacé*
Pair each of 2¾mm (UK No 12/US size 2) and 3¼mm
  (UK No 10/US size 3) knitting needles

SIZES AND MEASUREMENTS

To fit ages	2	3	4	years
Finished knitted measurements				
Around chest	73	78	83	cm
	28¾	30¾	32½	in
Length to shoulder	40	43	46	cm
	15¾	17	18	in
Sleeve length	24	28	31	cm
	9½	11	12¼	in

TENSION

25 sts and 34 rows to 10cm/4in over st st using 3¼mm
(UK No 10/US size 3) needles.

ABBREVIATIONS

See page 21.

BACK

With 2¾mm (No12/US 2) needles cast on 92(98:104) sts.
Work 7 rows in garter st (k every row) to form garter st band.
Change to 3¼mm (No 10/US 3) needles and work back with garter st edging for vents as foll:
Next row (RS) K to end.
Next row K5, p to last 5 sts, k5.
Rep last 2 rows 3 times more, so ending with a WS row.
Beg with a k row, work in st st only until back measures 38(41:44)cm/15(16¼:17¼)in from cast-on edge, ending with a WS (purl) row.
Shape Neck
Divide for neck shaping on next row as foll:
Next row (RS) K36(38:40), then turn, leaving rem sts on a spare needle.
Working on this set of sts only for first side of neck and cont in st st throughout, dec one st at neck edge on next 6 rows. 30(32:34) sts.
Work one row without shaping.
Cast off.
With RS facing, rejoin yarn to rem sts and cast off first 20(22:24) sts for centre back neck, then k to end.
Cont in st st throughout, dec one st at neck edge on next 6 rows. 30(32:34) sts.
Work 2 rows without shaping. Cast off.

FRONT

Work as given for back until front measures 28(30:32)cm/11(11¾:12½)in from cast-on edge, ending with a RS (knit) row.
Beg garter st edging for point of V-neck on next row as foll:
Next row (WS) P45(48:51), k2, p45(48:51).
Next row K to end.
Next row P44(47:50), k4, p44(47:50).
Next row K to end.
Next row P43(46:49), k6, p43(47:49).
Shape V-Neck
Divide for neck shaping on next row as foll:
Next row (RS) K46(49:52), then turn, leaving rem sts on a spare needle.
Working on this set of sts only for first side of neck, beg garter st neck edging and shaping as foll:
Next row (WS) K3, p to end.
Next row K to last 6 sts, k2tog, k4.
Rep last 2 rows until 33(35:37) sts rem, so ending with a RS row.
Next row (WS) K3, p to end.
Next row K to end.
Rep last 2 rows until front matches back to shoulder shaping, ending with a WS row (at armhole edge).
Next row (RS) Cast off first 30(32:34) sts, k to end.
Cont in garter st on 3 rem sts until band is long enough to fit around back neck edge to centre back neck.
Cast off.
With RS facing, rejoin yarn to rem sts, then k to end.
Next row (WS) P to last 3 sts, k3.
Next row K4, skpo, k to end.
Rep last 2 rows until 33(35:37) sts rem, so ending with a RS row.
Next row (WS) P to last 3 sts, k3.
Next row K to end.
Rep the last 2 rows until front matches back to shoulder shaping, ending with a RS row (at armhole edge).
Next row Cast off first 30(32:34), k to end.
Cont in garter st on 3 rem sts until band is long enough to fit around back neck to centre back neck. Cast off.

SLEEVES (make 2)

With 2¾mm (No 12/US 2) needles, cast on 42(46:50) sts.
Work 9 rows in garter st for cuff.
Change to 3¼mm (No 10/US 3) needles.
Beg with a k row, work in st st, inc one st at each end of next row and then every foll 3rd row until there are 90(94:98) sts.
Cont in st st, work without shaping until sleeve measures 24(28:31)cm/9½(11:12¼)in from cast-on edge. Cast off.

TO MAKE UP

Join both shoulder seams. Sew neckbands to back neck edge and join ends of neckbands at centre back neck. Sew on sleeves, matching centre of sleeve to shoulder seam.
Leaving side vents open along garter st edging at lower edge, join side and sleeve seams.

Baby's Top with Moss Stitch Trim

Knitted in a crisp cotton yarn, the moss stitch borders and bands show up beautifully on this simple baby's top, which also has small side vents at the lower edge of the garment. (See page 17 for more about moss stitch.)

MATERIALS

3(4:5) x 50g (1³/₄oz) balls of Jaeger *Pure Cotton*
Pair each of 2³/₄mm (UK No 12/ US size 2) and 3¹/₄mm
  (UK No 10/US size 3) knitting needles
3 buttons

SIZES AND MEASUREMENTS

To fit age	3–6	6–12	12–18 months
Finished knitted measurements			
Around chest	51	56	62	cm
	20	22	24¹/₂	in
Length to shoulder	26	30	35	cm
	10¹/₄	11³/₄	13³/₄	in
Sleeve length	15	18	22	cm
	6	7	8³/₄	in

TENSION

26 sts and 34 rows to 10cm/4in over st st using 3¹/₄mm
(UK No 10/US size 3) needles.

ABBREVIATIONS

See page 21.

BACK

With 2³/₄mm (No 12/ US 2) needles, cast on 67(73:81) sts.
Beg moss st band as foll:
1st moss st row K1, *p1, k1; rep from * to end.
Rep last row 3 times more.
Change to 3¹/₄mm (No 10/US 3) needles and work back with moss st edging for vents as foll:
Next row (RS) K1, p1, k to last 2 sts, p1, k1.
Next row K1, p1, k1, p to last 3 sts, k1, p1, k1.
Rep last 2 rows twice more, so ending with a WS row.
Beg with a k row, work in st st only until back measures 26(30:35)cm/10¹/₄(11³/₄:13³/₄) in from cast-on edge, ending with a WS (purl) row.
Shape Shoulders
Cast off 9(10:11) sts at beg of next 4 rows.
Leave rem 31(33:37) sts on a st holder for back neck.

FRONT

Work as given for back until front measures 13(17:20)cm/5¹/₄ (6³/₄:8)in from cast-on edge, ending with a WS (purl) row.

Neck Opening

Divide for neck opening on next row as foll:
Next row (RS) K31(34:38), then turn, leaving rem sts on a spare needle.
Working on this set of sts only for first side of neck, beg neck opening with moss st edging as foll:
Next row Cast on 5 sts at beg of row, then k1, [p1, k1] twice over these cast-on sts, p to end. 36(39:43) sts.
Next row (RS) K to last 4 sts, [p1, k1] twice.
Next row K1, [p1, k1] twice, p to end.
Rep last 2 rows 11(13:15) times more, so ending with a WS row.
Next row (RS) K to last 10(11:12) sts, slip these last 10(11:12) sts onto a safety pin. 26(28:31) sts.
Shape Neck
Cont in st st only, dec one st at neck edge on every foll row until 18(20:22) sts rem.
Work without shaping until front matches back to shoulder shaping, ending at armhole edge.
Shape Shoulder
Cast off 9(10:11) sts at beg of next row.
P one row.
Cast off rem 9(10:11) sts to complete first side of neck.
With RS facing, rejoin yarn to rem sts, [k1, p1] twice, then k to end.
Next row (WS) P to last 5 sts, k1, [p1, k1] twice.
Next row [K1, p1] twice, k to end.
Keeping to patt as set throughout (working 5 sts at neck edge

There is a wonderful range of yarn shades available now. Rather than pastels or beiges for babies, try neutrals, taupes or terracottas.

opening in moss st and rem sts in st st), work 5 rows more, so ending with a WS row.

Work first buttonhole on next row as foll:

Buttonhole row (RS) Work first 2 sts in moss st, work 2 sts tog, yf, k to end.

Work 9(11:13) rows without shaping, so ending with a WS row.

Work buttonhole row once more.

Work 7(9:11) rows without shaping, so ending with a WS row.

Shape Neck

Next row (RS) Work first 10(11:12) sts and slip these sts onto a safety pin, then k to end.

Cont in st st only, dec one st at neck edge on every foll row until 18(20:22) sts rem.

Work without shaping until front matches back to shoulder shaping, ending at armhole edge.

Shape Shoulder

Cast off 9(10:11) sts at beg of next row.

K one row.

Cast off rem 9(10:11) sts.

SLEEVES (make 2)

With 2³/₄mm (No 12/ US 2) needles, cast on 31(35:39) sts.

Work 6 rows in moss st as given for back.

Change to 3¹/₄mm (No10/US 3) needles.

Beg with a k row, work in st st, inc one st at each end of the 3rd(5th:1st) row and then every foll 3rd(3rd:4th) row until there are 55(63:71) sts.

Cont in st st throughout, work without shaping until sleeve measures 15(18:22)cm/ 6(7:8³/₄)in from cast-on edge, ending with a WS row.

Cast off.

NECKBAND

Join both shoulder seams.

Using 2³/₄mm (No 12/ US 2) needles, with RS facing and beg at right front neck, slip 10(11:12) sts from safety pin onto needle, pick up and k 14(16:18) sts evenly up right front neck, k 31(33:37) sts from back neck st holder, pick up and k 14(16:18) sts down left front neck, work across 10(11:12) sts from safety pin. 79(87:97) sts.

Work one row in moss st.

Work buttonhole on next row as foll:

Buttonhole row (RS) Work first 2 sts in moss st, work 2 sts tog, yf, work in moss st to end.

Work 3 rows in moss st.

Cast off in moss st.

TO MAKE UP

Sew on sleeves, matching centre of sleeves to shoulder seams.

Leaving side vents open along moss st edging at lower edge of garment, join side and sleeve seams.

Lap buttonhole band over button band and stitch lower edge in place. Sew on buttons.

The eyelet detailing is worked a few stitches in from the edge on the shaped sides and sleeves of this sweater. It creates decorative interest on the simple stocking stitch fabric.

Raglan Sweater with Funnel Neck

This semi-fitted sweater uses fully fashioned shaping for detailing. By working into the front of the stitch instead of the back for the 'make one' increases you create decorative eyelets.

MATERIALS

10(11:12) x 50g (1³/₄oz) balls of Rowan *All Seasons Cotton*
Pair of 4¹/₂mm (UK No 7/US size 7) knitting needles

SIZES AND MEASUREMENTS

To fit bust	82–87	87–92	92–97 cm
	32–34	34–36	36–38 in
Finished knitted measurements			
Around bust	88	94	102 cm
	34³/₄	37	40 in
Length to shoulder	54	58	61 cm
	21¹/₄	22³/₄	24 in
Sleeve length	43	44	45 cm
	17	17¹/₄	17³/₄ in

TENSION

18 sts and 25 rows to 10cm/4in over st st using 4¹/₂mm (UK No 7/US size 7) needles.

ABBREVIATIONS

See page 21.

BACK and FRONT (both alike)

With 4¹/₂mm (UK No 7/US size 7) needles, cast on 82(88:94) sts. Beg with a k row, work 10 rows in st st, so ending with a WS (purl) row.

Shape Sides

Beg side shaping on next row as foll:
Next row (RS) K3, skpo, k to last 5 sts, k2tog, k3.
Beg with a p row and cont in st st throughout, work 9 rows without shaping, so ending with a WS (purl) row.
Next row (RS) K3, skpo, k to last 5 sts, k2tog, k3.
Rep last 10 rows once more, so ending with a RS (knit) row. 76(82:88) sts.
Work 15 rows without shaping, so ending with a WS (purl) row.
Next row (RS) K3, pick up horizontal loop before next st with tip of left-hand needle and k into **front** of it to make a new st—called

make one or *m1—*, k to last 3 sts, m1, k3.

Rep last 16 rows once more. 80(86:92) sts.

Work without shaping until work measures 31(32:33)cm/12¼ (12½:13)in from cast-on edge, ending with a WS (purl) row.

Shape Raglan Armholes

Beg armhole shaping on next row as foll:

Next row (RS) K3, skpo, k to last 5 sts, k2tog, k3.

Next row P to end.

Next row K3, skpo, k to last 5 sts, k2tog, k3.

Rep last 2 rows until 30 sts rem, so ending with a RS (knit) row.

Work 13 rows without shaping.

Cast off.

SLEEVES (make 2)

With 4½mm (UK No 7/US size 7) needles, cast on 40(42:44) sts.

Beg with a k row, work 10(14:12) rows in st st, so ending with a WS (purl) row.

Cont in st st throughout, beg shaping sleeve on next row as foll:

Next row (RS) K3, m1, k to last 3 sts, m1, k3.

Work 7(5:5) rows without shaping, so ending with a WS (purl) row.

Next row (RS) K3, m1, k to last 3 sts, m1, k3.

Rep last 8(6:6) rows until there are 64(70:76) sts.

Work without shaping until sleeve measures 43(44:45)cm/17 (17¼:17¾)in from cast-on edge, ending with a WS (purl) row.

Shape Raglan Top

Beg shaping raglan sleeve top on next row as foll:

Next row (RS) K3, skpo, k to last 5 sts, k2tog, k3.

Next row P to end.

Next row K3, skpo, k to last 5 sts, k2tog, k3.

Rep last 2 rows until 14 sts rem, so ending with a RS (knit) row.

Work 13 rows without shaping.

Cast off.

TO MAKE UP

Join raglan seams. Join side and sleeve seams.

The funnel neck runs up from the main part of the sweater, creating a pretty neckline that stands away form the neck. As the top sleeve seams on a raglan design show, use mattress stitch for a perfect invisible seam.

Knitted Textures

Knitting is the perfect medium to create beautiful textural detail, from basic stitches to intricate cabling

Knitted textures basics

The two most frequently used techniques for creating heavily textured knitted fabrics are making cables and making bobbles. The instructions for the simple bobbles and cables that follow will provide you with the basis for working their many variations. My classes on Aran designs on pages 42–45 covers more specialized textured stitches methods and tips.

Cables

Knitted cables are formed by crossing one set of stitches over another. This is done by leaving stitches on a cable needle at the back of the knitting (creating a cable that crosses to the right) or at the front of the knitting (creating a cable that crosses to the left). A cable needle is a short double-pointed needle. The cable needles I prefer to work with have a curve in the middle to prevent the stitches from falling off. The cable examples that follow are worked over six stitches, but cables can be worked over a smaller or larger amount of stitches. (See the Cable Cushion on page 50, where a 4-stitch cable has been used.)

BACK CROSS CABLE

1 Slip the first three cable stitches purlwise off the left-hand needle and onto the cable needle. Leave the cable needle at the back of the work, then knit the next three stitches on the left-hand needle, keeping the yarn tight to prevent a gap from forming in the knitting.

2 Next, knit the three stitches directly from the cable needle, or if preferred, slip the three stitches from the cable needle back onto the left-hand needle and then knit them. This completes the cable cross.

FRONT CROSS CABLE

1 Slip the first three cable stitches purlwise off the left-hand needle and onto the cable needle. Leave the cable needle at the front of the work, then knit the next three stitches on the left-hand needle, keeping the yarn tight to prevent a gap from forming in the knitting.

2 Knit the three stitches directly from the cable needle, or if preferred, slip the three stitches from the cable needle back onto the left-hand needle and then knit them. This completes the cable cross.

Bobbles

A bobble is created by working increases into one stitch and then reducing them back to one stitch once it is completed. Two versions are shown here – one worked over one row and the other over several, turning rows. Both can be made bigger or smaller by working fewer or more stitches, or fewer or more rows. Although these bobbles are shown worked on a stocking stitch background, you could also work them on reverse stocking stitch. The multi-row bobble can be worked in either stocking stitch (as it is here) or in reverse stocking stitch for a different texture; to do this work your first row after the first turning (step 2) as a knit or a purl row.

ONE-ROW BOBBLE

1 To make four bobble stitches from one stitch, knit into the front of the next stitch in the usual way, then knit into the back, the front and the back of the same stitch before slipping it off the left-hand needle (see 'inc one' on page 18 for how this is done). Lift the second stitch on the right-hand needle over the first stitch and off the needle as shown.

2 Then take the third and fourth stitches over the first stitch and off the needle in the same way, one at a time. This decreases the four stitches back to the one stitch and completes the one-row bobble.

MULTI-ROW BOBBLE ('make bobble')

1 To make five bobble stitches from one stitch, knit into the front of the next stitch in the usual way, then knit into the back, the front, the back and the front of the same stitch before slipping it off the left-hand needle (see 'inc one' on page 18 for how this is done).

2 Turn your knitting and purl the five bobble stitches, then turn and knit the five stitches. Work one more purl row and one more knit row on these same stitches, so your last row is a right-side row.

3 With the right side still facing, insert the point of the left-hand needle in the second stitch on the right-hand needle and take it over the first stitch and off the needle. Then do the same with the third, fourth and fifth stitches, one at a time, to complete the bobble.
(A variation of this can be made by working the third and fourth turning rows thus: p2tog, p1, p2tog, turn, slip 1, k2tog, psso.)

Cable panels class

I love texture. I love the fact that by putting cables, bobbles and raised stitches together you can create your own unique knitted landscape. Here are some guidelines for how to do just that.

How to choose Aran panels

When starting to design an Aran knit, I begin by sketching out simple shapes and then filling them in with linear details of stitch patterns. I like to instil a harmony in the design, and feel that the best way to achieve this is to choose stitch panels that link in some way. It may simply be that a moss stitch centre to a diamond-shaped cable is carried over to moss stitch welts and selvedge borders, or that all the cables and ribs are created by knitting into the back of the stitches, giving them more definition.

The swatches here show the design process behind the Lace Denim Tunic that appeared in my book *Family Collection*. First I chose a denim cotton yarn that does not fade like the blue version, but that shows up textured stitch patterns beautifully. It is a heavy yarn, however, so to create a more delicate openwork look I decided to introduce lace stitches in the design.

For me, the design process always begins with knitting up each of my selected stitch patterns in a separate swatch. This is important because these individual swatches can then be positioned and repositioned next to one another until the best sequence is achieved. I even knit the four-stitch and six-stitch cable panels that I will use to divide the larger cables to see which one works best with the proportions of the other patterns. A six-stitch cable may look too heavy, or a four-stitch one too insignificant in relation to the panels next to them.

For the Denim Lace Tunic, I first knitted the central panel – a pattern with beautiful lace diagonals that also created a slight trellis effect. I wanted the other panels to echo this, so I chose ones that had lace diagonals or chevrons, and cables that also had a woven or trellis look. I felt it was important to then add a pretty, but not too lacy, lower border to the tunic. The Chevron Lace edging, knitted onto the bottom of the swatches was perfect. It created a scalloped effect that also worked well at the bottom of the sleeve and as a neckband. (See page 105 for instructions for Chevron Lace.)

Practising Aran textures

In the Aran Throw on page 51, I have used traditional stitch patterns in a patchwork of texture. You could isolate the squares and knit them separately to practise all the components of Aran design. There are vertical cables, travelling cables (where the cable is worked to the left or the right) and bobbles. You will notice that the squares when worked together in the throw are not perfect. This is because the cables pull in more in some squares than others, distorting the shape of the patches. To be perfect, increasings and decreasings would have to have been worked after each horizontal line of patches to compensate for this slight distortion. However, I felt that if you were a knitter that had not tackled such a large piece as this before, you may have been daunted by the idea of working 'shaping rows' as well. As the throw will be probably be draped casually over a bed or sofa, no one hopefully will care!

Designing your own Aran sweater

To design your own Aran sweater, choose your stitch pattern panels and knit them up as swatches. Then arrange the panels, selecting one for the centre and the others fanning out from it. In your final sequence you will repeat the panels on the right of the centre panel, on the left of that panel. When you find a sequence that you like, you can look for a suitable border. You may find a border in the Edgings chapter that then works really well with your panels.

Measure the distance from the centre of the panel that you have chosen for the middle of your design, out to the outside edge of your first panel. See if this is half the actual width of the garment you want to make. Then add more panels or take away panels if you need to, until you achieve the measurement that you need. Keep your sweater shape simple – a tunic shape with straight sides, and dropped shoulders will be ideal. (See the Simple Shaping Class on pages 26 and 27.)

Position your front neck with care. Try not to work your cable crosses just prior to where your neck shaping starts, as this can distort your neckline. On the sleeves, you will find that you can only place a certain amount of stitch panels after your cuff, or your sleeve width at the bottom will be too wide. This means that as you increase up the length of the sleeves you will need to add stitches into a simple stitch pattern. Use one that has an interesting stitch texture, such as double moss stitch, rather than reverse stocking stitch, which can look flat and rather 'bare'.

Texture detailing class

Once you have designed a series of panels for an Aran sweater, you can give it an extra-special look by detailing with the perfect borders, cuffs, neckband or collar. By taking the time to do this you will make your own design more personal, and certainly more original than ready-to-wear or mass-produced knitwear.

Carrying the textures into the borders

Textured knits usually look much nicer if stitch patterns from the main part of the design are also carried through into welts. This can mean at its simplest that a rib that may separate cables is also carried down into the ribs of the welt, or that a four-stitch cable in the body is also included in the ribs. In the Cabled Sweater on page 59, I felt it was really important that some of the complex stitch patterns on the sweater were also part of the double rib borders at the bottom of the body and sleeves. Adding them to the deep neckband also helped to create a more rigid collar that stands away from the neck.

A more dramatic effect can be created by running a large centre pattern panel down into the lower welt and up into the neckband, or by having no lower border at all, thus giving it an unstructured look. If bobbles are used in a main pattern and it does not make the design too over-the-top by doing so, you could also try introducing a small bobble in the purl stitches of the ribs.

Adding extra stitches to compensate for cables

This does, however, draw attention to the fact that cables will draw in the knitted fabric. If, for instance, you were customizing a simple sweater by introducing a centre cable panel, you would notice that the actual width of the piece is narrowed by the cable. To prevent this, knitting designers usually compensate by increasing to more stitches after a lower border is completed and before the cable pattern is started. This does, unfortunately, make it more difficult when you are running patterns down into your borders, since you need to work your increases in places that do not then affect the continuity of those patterns.

Yarns and Aran textures

Different yarns and weights produce different effects – a fine cotton yarn can give crisp, sharp stitch detailing which can look perfect on a neat, textured summer jacket, but a thicker cotton yarn can add too much weight to a generous Aran-style tunic. A double knitting wool rarely gives the stitch detail I like, so I tend to work in an Aran-weight wool. One of my favourite yarns has to be a denim yarn that fades as it is washed and worn. As it fades on textured designs the colour change can highlight the more raised stitches, giving them added depth. The garment then becomes more beautiful as time goes on.

> ### CABLE NEEDLE TIP
> For best results, use a cable needle that is slightly smaller than the main needles so that the stitches do not stretch.

Moss Stitch Jacket

Moss stitch is my favourite stitch. It is important to use a good-quality wool or cotton yarn to maintain stitch clarity. This boxy style has turned back cuffs.

MATERIALS

9(10:11) x 100g (3½oz) hanks of Rowan *Magpie Aran*
Pair each of 3¾mm (UK No 9/US size 5) and 4½mm
   (UK No 7/US size 7) knitting needles
8 buttons

SIZES AND MEASUREMENTS

To fit	small	medium	large	
Finished knitted measurements				
Around bust	104	108	112	cm
	41	42½	44	in
Length to shoulder	48	50	52	cm
	19	19¾	20½	in
Sleeve length (with cuff turned back)				
	43	46	48	cm
	17	18	19	in

TENSION

18 sts and 32 rows to 10cm/4in over moss st using 4½mm
(UK No 7/US size 7) needles.

ABBREVIATIONS

See page 21.

BACK

With 3¾mm (No 9/US 5) needles, cast on 95(99:103) sts.
Work 7 rows in garter st (k every row) to form garter st band.
Change to 4½mm (No 7/US 7) needles and beg moss st patt as foll:
1st moss st row (RS) K1, *p1, k1; rep from * to end. (Mark this row as RS with a coloured thread.)
Rep last row to form moss st patt, cont in moss st until back measures 48(50:52)cm/19(19¾:20½)in from cast-on edge, ending with a WS row.
Shape Shoulders
Keeping patt correct as set and casting off in patt, cast off 15(15:16) sts at beg of next 2 rows and 15(16:16) sts at beg of foll 2 rows.
Cast off rem 35(37:39) sts.

POCKET LININGS (make 2)

With 4½mm (No 7/US 7) needles, cast on 23 sts.
Work in moss st as given for back until pocket measures 12cm/4¾in from cast-on edge.
Leave sts on a st holder.

LEFT FRONT

With 3¾mm (No 9/US No 5) needles, cast on 49(51:53) sts.
Work 7 rows in garter st to form garter st band.
Change to 4½mm (No 7/US 7) needles and beg moss st patt with garter st button band as foll:
Next row (RS) P1, *k1, p1; rep from * to last 4 sts, k4. (Mark this row as RS with a coloured thread.)
Next row K4, *p1, k1; rep from * to last st, p1.
Rep last 2 rows until front measures 12cm/4¾in *from beg of moss st patt*, ending with a WS row.
Place Pocket
Keeping moss st patt correct as set, place pocket on next row as foll:
Next row (RS) Work first 13(15:17) sts in moss st; slip next 23 sts onto a st holder, then holding pocket lining at back of work, work in moss st across 23 sts of pocket lining from st holder; work 9 sts in moss st, k4.
Cont in patt at set (working front in moss st with 4-st garter st button band) until front measures 40(41:42)cm/15¾(16:16½)in from cast-on edge, ending with a WS row.
Shape Neck
Beg neck shaping on next row as foll:
Next row (RS) Work in moss st to last 9 sts, then slip last 9 sts onto a st holder.
Cont in moss st throughout, dec one st at neck edge on every foll row until 30(31:32) sts rem.
Work without shaping until front matches back to shoulder shaping, ending at armhole edge.
Shape Shoulder
Casting off in patt, cast off 15(15:16) sts at beg of next row.
Work one row without shaping.
Cast off rem 15(16:16) sts.
Mark positions of buttons on button band, the first one on first row of moss st above garter st band at bottom of left front, the last one 1cm/½in from neck edge and the rem 6 evenly spaced between.

RIGHT FRONT

With 3¾mm (No 9/US No 5) needles, cast on 49(51:53) sts.
Work 7 rows in garter st to form garter st band.
Change to 4½mm (No 7/US 7) needles.
Beg moss st patt with garter st buttonhole band, working first buttonhole as foll:
Next row (buttonhole row) (RS) K1, k2 tog, yf, k1, *p1, k1; rep from * to last st, p1. (Mark this buttonhole row as RS with a coloured thread.)
Next row P1, *k1, p1; rep from * to last 4 sts, k4.
Next row K4, *p1, k1; rep from * to last st, p1.
Next row P1, *k1, p1; rep from * to last 4 sts, k4.

Rep last 2 rows working buttonholes when reached **and at the same time** when right front matches left front to pocket placement, place pocket as foll:

Next row (RS) K4, work 9 sts in moss st; slip next 23 sts onto a st holder, then holding pocket lining at back of work, work in moss st across 23 sts of pocket lining from st holder; work rem 13(15:17) sts in moss st.

Cont in patt at set (working front in moss st with 4-st garter st buttonhole band), working buttonholes when reached, until right front matches left front to neck shaping, ending with a WS row.

Shape Neck

Beg neck shaping on next row as foll:

Next row (RS) K4, work next 5 sts in moss st and then slip these first 9 sts onto a st holder, work in moss st to end.

Complete to match left front, reversing neck and shoulder shapings.

POCKET TOPS (both alike)

Using 3¾mm (No 9/US 5) needles and with RS facing, k across 23 sts of pocket from st holder.

K 3 rows.

Cast off knitwise.

SLEEVES (make 2)

With 4½mm (No 7/US 7) needles, cast on 45(47:49) sts.

Work 7cm/2¾in moss st as given for back.

Change to 3¾mm (No 9/US 5) needles and work 7cm/2¾in more in moss st.

Change back to 4½mm (No 7/US 7) needles.

Keeping to moss st as set throughout and working new sts into moss st patt, inc one st at each end of next row and then every foll 6th row until there are 79(83:87) sts.

Work without shaping until sleeve measures 50(53:55)cm/19¾ (20¾:21¾)in from cast-on edge.

Cast off in patt.

The pocket linings for this jacket are worked first, and then integrated into the fronts. This looks a lot neater than sewing on patch pockets afterwards.

COLLAR

Join shoulder seams.

Using 3³/₄mm (No 9/US 5) needles, with RS facing and beg at right front neck, slip 9 sts from st holder onto needle, pick up and k 18(20:22) sts evenly up right front neck, 35(37:39) sts across back neck, 18(20:22) sts down left front neck, work 9 sts from st holder in patt as set. 89(95:101) sts.

1st row (WS) K4, work in moss st to last 4 sts, k4.

2nd row (RS) Cast off first 3 sts knitwise, work in moss st to last 4 sts, k4.

3rd row Cast off first 3 sts knitwise, work in moss st to end. 83(89:95) sts.

4th row K4, work 59(63:67) sts in moss st, turn leaving rem sts unworked.

5th row Work 43(45:47) sts in moss st, turn.

6th row Work 47(49:51) sts in moss st, turn.

7th row Work 51(53:55) sts in moss st, turn.

8th row Work 55(57:59) sts in moss st, turn.

9th row Work 59(61:63) sts in moss st, turn.

10th row Work 63(65:67) sts in moss st, turn.

11th row Work 67(69:71) sts in moss st, turn.

12th row Work in moss st to last 4 sts, k4.

Working new sts into moss st patt, cont as foll:

13th row K4, m1, work in moss st to last 4 sts, m1, k4. 85(91:97) sts.

14th, 15th and 16th rows K4, work in moss st to last 4 sts, k4.

Rep the last 4 rows (13th–16th rows) 4 times more. 93(99:105) sts.

K 4 rows.

Cast off knitwise.

TO MAKE UP

Sew on sleeves, matching centre of sleeve to shoulder seam. Join side and sleeve seams, reversing seam for cuff turnback. Catch down pocket linings and sides of pocket tops. Sew on buttons.

Using a reversible fabric, such as moss stitch or garter stitch, means you can introduce simple design details like a turned back cuff on the sleeves.

Cable Cushion

Making a cabled cushion cover is an ideal way to practise and perfect your cabling technique. Use a good-quality wool yarn to ensure elasticity.

MATERIALS

2 x 100g (3¹/₂oz) hanks of Rowan *Magpie Aran*
Pair of 4¹/₂mm (UK No 7/US size 7) knitting needles
Cable needle
4 buttons
Cushion pad 35cm x 35cm/14in x14in

MEASUREMENTS

Approximate size 35 x 36cm/14 x 14¹/₄in

TENSION

21 sts and 30 rows to 10cm/4in over patt (slightly stretched) using 4¹/₂mm (UK No 7/US size 7) needles.

ABBREVIATIONS

C4B (cable 4 back) = slip next 2 sts onto a cable needle and leave at back of work, k2, then k2 from cable needle.
See also page 21.

BACK OF COVER

With 4¹/₂mm (No 7/US 7) needles, cast on 74 sts.
Beg cable patt as foll:
1st patt row (RS) K2, *p1, k4, p1, k2; rep from * to end.
2nd patt row P2, *k1, p4, k1, p2; rep from * to end.
3rd patt row K2, *p1, C4B, p1, k2; rep from * to end.
4th patt row As row 2.
5th and 6th patt rows As rows 1 and 2.
The last 6 rows form the cable patt. Rep these 6 rows until back measures 33cm/13in from cast-on edge, ending with a WS row.
Button Band
Beg k2, p2 ribbing for button band as foll:
1st rib row (RS) K2, *p2, k2; rep from * to end.
2nd rib row P2, *k2, p2; rep from * to end.**
Rep last 2 rows twice more.
Cast off in rib.

FRONT OF COVER

Work as given for back to **.
Keeping to rib as set, work buttonholes over next two rows as foll:
1st buttonhole row (RS) Work first 9 sts in rib, cast off next 2 sts, [work in rib until there are 16 sts on needle after last cast-off, cast off next 2 sts] 3 times, work in rib to end.
2nd buttonhole row Rib to end, casting on 2 sts over those cast off in previous row.
Work 2 rows more in rib.
Cast off in rib.

TO MAKE UP

With right sides together, join three sides of cushion cover, leaving buttonhole-end open. Turn right side out.
Sew buttons to button band to correspond to buttonholes.

Aran Throw

This cabled throw uses all the techniques you need to know to work Aran designs. It creates a textured landscape of bobbles, cables, moss stitch and reverse stocking stitch.

MATERIALS
15 x 50g (1³/₄oz) balls of Jaeger *Matchmaker Merino Aran*
One each of 4mm (UK No 8/US size 6) and 4¹/₂mm
  (UK No 7/US size 7) long circular knitting needles
Cable needle

MEASUREMENTS
Approximate size 74 x 102cm/29 x 40in

TENSION
20 sts and 36 rows to 10cm/4in over moss st using 4¹/₂mm
(UK No 7/US size 7) needles.

ABBREVIATIONS
C6F (cable 6 front) = slip next 3 sts onto a cable needle and leave at front of work, k3, then k3 from cable needle.
C6B (cable 6 back) = slip next 3 sts onto a cable needle and leave at back of work, k3, then k3 from cable needle.
C5F (cross 5 front) = slip next 3 sts onto a cable needle and leave at front of work, k2, then slip the p st from cable needle back onto left-hand needle, p this st, then k2 from cable needle.
T3F (twist 3 front) = slip next 2 sts onto a cable needle and leave at front of work, p1, then k2 from cable needle.
T3B (twist 3 back) = slip next st onto a cable needle and leave at back of work, k2, then p1 from cable needle.
T4F (twist 4 front) = slip next 2 sts onto a cable needle and leave at front of work, p2, then k2 from cable needle.
T4B (twist 4 back) = slip next 2 sts onto a cable needle and leave at back of work, k2, then p2 from cable needle.
C4F (cable 4 front) = slip next 2 sts onto a cable needle and leave at front of work, k2, then k2 from cable needle.
C4B (cable 4 back) = slip next 2 sts onto a cable needle and leave at back of work, k2, then k2 from cable needle.
T5F (twist 5 front) = slip next 3 sts onto a cable needle and leave at front of work, p2, then k3 from cable needle.
T5B (twist 5 back) = slip next 2 sts onto a cable needle and leave at back of work, k3, then p2 from cable needle.
T5L (twist 5 left) = slip next 2 sts onto a cable needle and leave at front of work, k2, p1, then k2 from cable needle.
See also page 21.

MOTIF PATTERNS
The following are the motifs used for the patterned squares on the Aran Throw:

Motif A (worked over 34 sts)
1st row (RS) [P1, k1] 3 times, p1, k6, p1, [p1, k1] 3 times, p1, k6, p1, [k1, p1] 3 times.
2nd row [P1, k1] 3 times, k1, p6, k1, [k1, p1] 3 times, k1, p6, k1, [k1, p1] 3 times.
3rd–6th rows Rep 1st and 2nd rows twice more.
7th row [P1, k1] 3 times, p1, C6F, p1, [p1, k1] 3 times, p1, C6F, p1, [k1, p1] 3 times.
8th row As 2nd row.
9th–38th rows Rep 1st–8th rows 3 times more, then 1st–6th rows again.

Motif B (worked over 34 sts)

1st row (RS) P7, C5F, p10, C5F, p7.

2nd row K7, p2, k1, p2, k10, p2, k1, p2, k7.

3rd row P6, T3B, k1, T3F, p8, T3B, k1, T3F, p6.

4th row K6, p2, k1, p1, k1, p2, k8, p2, k1, p1, k1, p2, k6.

5th row P5, T3B, k1, p1, k1, T3F, p6, T3B, k1, p1, k1, T3F, p5.

6th row K5, p2, [k1, p1] twice, k1, p2, k6, p2, [k1, p1] twice, k1, p2, k5.

7th row P4, T3B, [k1, p1] twice, k1, T3F, p4, T3B, [k1, p1] twice, k1, T3F, p4.

8th row K4, p2, [k1, p1] 3 times, k1, p2, k4, p2, [k1, p1] 3 times, k1, p2, k4.

9th row P3, T3B, [k1, p1] 3 times, k1, T3F, p2, T3B, [k1, p1] 3 times, k1, T3F, p3.

10th row K3, p2, [k1, p1] 4 times, k1, p2, k2, p2, [k1, p1] 4 times, k1, p2, k3.

11th row P3, T3F, [p1, k1] 3 times, p1, T3B, p2, T3F, [p1, k1] 3 times, p1, T3B, p3.

12th row As 8th row.

13th row P4, T3F, [p1, k1] twice, p1, T3B, p4, T3F, [p1, k1] twice, p1, T3B, p4.

14th row As 6th row.

15th row P5, T3F, p1, k1, p1, T3B, p6, T3F, p1, k1, p1, T3B, p5.

16th row As 4th row.

17th row P6, T3F, p1, T3B, p8, T3F, p1, T3B, p6.

18th row As 2nd row.

19th–38th rows Rep 1st–18th rows once more, then 1st and 2nd rows again.

Motif C (worked over 34 sts)

1st row (RS) P1, k1, p3, k2, p8, C4B, p8, k2, p3, k1, p1.

2nd row P1, k1, p1, k2, p2, k8, p4, k8, p2, k2, p1, k1, p1.

3rd row P1, k1, p3, T4F, p4, T4B, T4F, p4, T4B, p3, k1, p1.

4th row P1, k1, p1, k4, [p2, k4] 3 times, p2, k4, p1, k1, p1.

5th row P1, k1, p5, T4F, T4B, p4, T4F, T4B, p5, k1, p1.

6th row P1, k1, p1, k6, p4, k8, p4, k6, p1, k1, p1.

7th row P1, k1, p7, C4B, p4; pick up horizontal loop between st just worked and next st with tip of left-hand needle and k into front, back and front of it, [turn and k3] 3 times, turn and sl 1, k2tog, psso, p1, then psso again—called *make bobble* or *MB*—; p3, C4F, p7, k1, p1.

8th row As 6th row.

9th row P1, k1, p5, T4B, T4F, p4, T4B, T4F, p5, k1, p1.

10th row As 4th row.

11th row P1, k1, p3, T4B, p4, T4F, T4B, p4, T4F, p3, k1, p1.

12th row As 2nd row.

13th row P1, k1, p3, k2, p4, MB, p4, C4B, p4, MB, p4, k2, p3, k1, p1.

14th row P1, k1, p1, k2, p2, k8, p4, k8, p2, k2, p1, k1, p1.

15th–26th rows Rep 3rd–14th rows once more.

27th–36th rows Rep 3rd–12th rows.

37th and 38th rows As 1st and 2nd rows.

Motif D (worked over 34 sts)

1st row (RS) P1, k1, p4, T3B, p5, C6B, p5, T3F, p4, k1, p1.

2nd row P1, k1, p1, k3, p2, k6, p6, k6, p2, k3, p1, k1, p1.

3rd row P1, k1, p3, T3B, p4, T5B, T5F, p4, T3F, p3, k1, p1.

4th row P1, k1, p1, k2, p2, k5, p3, k4, p3, k5, p2, k2, p1, k1, p1.

5th row P1, k1, p2, T3B, p3, T5B, p4, T5F, p3, T3F, p2, k1, p1.

6th row [P1, k1] twice, p2, k1; k into front, back and front of next st, [turn and k3] 3 times, turn and sl 1, k2tog, psso—called *make bobble* or *MB*—; k2, p3, k8, p3, k2, MB, k1, p2, [k1, p1] twice.

7th row P1, k1, p2, T3F, p3, k3, p8, k3, p3, T3B, p2, k1, p1.

8th row P1, k1, p1, k2, p2, k3, p3, k8, p3, k3, p2, k2, p1, k1, p1.

9th row P1, k1, p3, T3F, p2, T5F, p4, T5B, p2, T3B, p3, k1, p1.

10th row P1, k1, p1, k3, p2, [k4, p3] twice, k4, p2, k3, p1, k1, p1.

11th row P1, k1, p4, T3F, p3, T5F, T5B, p3, T3B, p4, k1, p1.

12th row P1, k1, p1, k2, MB, k1, p2, k5, p6, k5, p2, k1, MB, k2, p1, k1, p1.

13th–38th rows Rep 1st–12th rows twice more, then 1st and 2nd rows again.

Motif E (worked over 34 sts)

1st row (RS) [P1, k1] 4 times, p3, k12, p3, [k1, p1] 4 times.

2nd row [P1, k1] 4 times, p1, k2, p12, k2, p1, [k1, p1] 4 times.

3rd and 4th rows As 1st and 2nd rows.

5th row [P1, k1] 4 times, p3, C6B, C6F, p3, [k1, p1] 4 times.

6th row As 2nd row.

7th and 8th rows Rep 1st and 2nd rows once more.

9th–38th rows Rep 1st–8th rows 3 times more, then 1st–6th rows again.

Motif F (worked over 34 sts)

1st row (RS) *P6, T5L, p6*; rep from * to * once more.

2nd row *K6, p2, k1, p2, k6*; rep from * to * once more.

3rd row *P5, T3B, k1, T3F, p5*; rep from * to * once more.

4th row *K5, p2, k1, p1, k1, p2, k5*; rep from * to * once more.

5th row *P4, T3B, k1, p1, k1, T3F, p4*; rep from * to * once more.

6th row *K4, p2, [k1, p1] twice, k1, p2, k4*; rep from * to * once more.

7th row *P3, T3B, [k1, p1] twice, k1, T3F, p3*; rep from * to * once more.

8th row *K3, p2, [k1, p1] 3 times, k1, p2, k3*; rep from * to * once more.

9th row *P2, T3B, [k1, p1] 3 times, k1, T3F, p2*; rep from * to * once more.

10th row *K2, p2, [k1, p1] 4 times, k1, p2, k2*; rep from * to * once more.

11th row *P1, T3B, [k1, p1] 4 times, k1, T3F, p1*; rep from * to * once more.

12th row *K1, p2, [k1, p1] 5 times, k1, p2, k1*; rep from * to * once more.

13th–38th rows Rep 1st–12th rows twice more, then 1st and 2nd rows again.

TO MAKE

With 4mm (No 8/US 6) circular needle, cast on 188 sts.
K 4 rows to form garter st edging.

Band 1

Change to 4¹/₂mm (No 7/US 7) circular needle and beg patt for first band of 5 square patches as foll:

1st row (RS) K3, work 1st row of Motif A, k3, work 1st row of Motif B, k3, work 1st row of Motif A, k3, work 1st row of Motif C, k3, work 1st row of Motif A, k3.

2nd row K3, work 2nd row of Motif A, k3, work 2nd row of Motif C, k3, work 2nd row of Motif A, k3, work 2nd row of Motif B, k3, work 2nd row of Motif A, k3.

These last 2 rows set the patt.

Cont in patt as set until 38 rows of motifs have been worked.
Change to 4mm (No 8/US 6) circular needle.

39th–42nd rows K 4 rows.

Band 2

Change to 4¹/₂mm (No 7/US 7) circular needle and beg patt for 2nd band of 5 square patches as foll:

43rd row (RS) K3, work 1st row of Motif D, k3, work 1st row of Motif E, k3, work 1st row of Motif F, k3, work 1st row of Motif E, k3, work 1st row of Motif D, k3.

44th row K3, work 2nd row of Motif D, k3, work 2nd row of Motif E, k3, work 2nd row of Motif F, k3, work 2nd row of Motif E, k3, work 2nd row of Motif D, k3.

These last 2 rows set the patt.

Cont in patt as set until 38 rows of motifs have been worked.
Change to 4mm (No 8/US 6) circular needle.

81st–84th rows K 4 rows.

Band 3

Change to 4¹/₂mm (No 7/US 7) circular needle and beg patt for 3rd band of 5 square patches as foll:

85th row (RS) K3, work 1st row of Motif A, k3, work 1st row of Motif C, k3, work 1st row of Motif A, k3, work 1st row of Motif B, k3, work 1st row of Motif A, k3.

86th row K3, work 2nd row of Motif A, k3, work 2nd row of Motif B, k3, work 2nd row of Motif A, k3, work 2nd row of Motif C, k3, work 2nd row of Motif A, k3.

These last 2 rows set the patt.

Cont in patt as set until 38 rows of motifs have been worked.
Change to 4mm (No 8/US 6) circular needle.

123rd–126th rows K 4 rows.

Band 4

Change to 4¹/₂mm (No7/US 7) circular needle and beg patt for 4th band of 5 square patches as foll:

127th row (RS) K3, work 1st row of Motif F, k3, work 1st row of Motif E, k3, work 1st row of Motif D, k3, work 1st row of Motif E, k3, work 1st row of Motif F, k3.

128th row K3, work 2nd row of Motif F, k3, work 2nd row of Motif E, k3, work 2nd row of Motif D, k3, work 2nd row of Motif E, k3, work 2nd row of Motif F, k3.

These last 2 rows set the patt.

Cont in patt as set until 38 rows of motifs have been worked.
Change to 4mm (No 8/US 6) circular needle.

165th–168th rows K 4 rows.

Change to 4¹/₂mm (No 7/US 7) circular needle.

169th–336th rows As 1st–168th rows.

Cast off.

Because of the number of stitches in this textured patchwork throw, a circular needle is required, but the rows are worked backwards and forwards.

Child's Guernsey with Hood

A practical hooded top with Guernsey patterning, this tunic would look equally good in a crisp navy or denim shade.

MATERIALS

9(11) x 50g (1³/₄oz) balls of Rowan *Cotton Glacé*
Pair each of 3mm (UK No 11/US size 2) and 3¹/₄mm
  (UK No 10/US size 3) knitting needles
Cable needle

SIZES AND MEASUREMENTS

To fit	3–4	5–6	years
Finished knitted measurements			
Around chest	80	94	cm
	31¹/₂	37	in
Length to shoulder	44	50	cm
	17¹/₄	19³/₄	in
Sleeve length	27	30	cm
	10¹/₂	11³/₄	in

TENSION

25 sts and 34 rows to 10cm/4in over st st using 3¹/₄mm
(UK No 10/US size 3) needles.

ABBREVIATIONS

C6F (cable 6 front) = slip next 3 sts onto a cable needle and leave at front of work, k3, then k3 from cable needle.
C6B (cable 6 back) = slip next 3 sts onto a cable needle and leave at back of work, k3, then k3 from cable needle.
See also page 21.

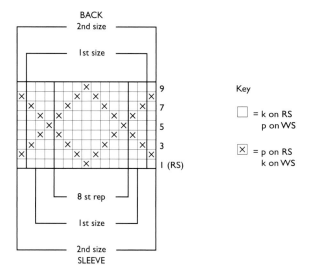

SPECIAL CHART NOTE

Read the chart from right to left on RS (odd-numbered) rows and from left to right on WS (even-numbered) rows.

PANEL PATTERNS

The following are the panel patts used on the tunic:

Panel A (worked over 13 sts)
1st row (RS) K13.
2nd row P13.
3th row K6, p1, k6.
4th row P5, k1, p1, k5.
5th row K4, p1, k3, p1, k4.
6th row P3, k1, [p2, k1] twice, p3.
7th row K2, p1, k2, p1, k1, p1, k2, p1, k2.
8th row P1, k1, p2, k1, p3, k1, p2, k1, p1.
9th row K3, p1, [k2, p1] twice, k3.
10th row P2, k1, p2, k1, p1, k1, p2, k1, p2.
11th row K4, p1, k3, p1, k4.
12th row P3, k1, [p2, k1] twice, p3.
13th row K5, p1, k1, p1, k5.
14th row P4, k1, p3, k1, p4.
15th row K6, p1, k6.
16th row P5, k1, p1, k1, p5.
17th row K6, p1, k6.
18th–22nd rows P13.
These 22 rows form the patt and are repeated throughout.

Panel B (worked over 10 sts)
1st row (RS) P1, k1, p1, k4, p1, k1, p1.
2nd row P1, k1, p6, k1, p1.
3rd row P1, k1, p1, C4F, p1, k1, p1.
4th row P1, k1, p6, k1, p1.
These 4 rows form the patt and are repeated throughout.

Panel C (worked over 13 sts)
1st row (RS) K13.
2nd row P13.
3rd row K6, p1, k6.
4th row P5, k1, p1, k1, p5.
5th row K4, p1, [k1, p1] twice, k4.
6th row P3, k1, [p1, k1] 3 times, p3.
7th row K2, p1, [k1, p1] 4 times, k2.
8th row P1, [k1, p1] 6 times.
9th row As row 7.
10th row As row 6.
11th row As row 5.
12th row As row 4.
13th row As row 3.
14th row P13.
These 14 rows form the patt and are repeated throughout.

Panel D (worked over 10 sts)
1st row (RS) P1, k1, p1, k4, p1, k1, p1.
2nd row P1, k1, p6, k1, p1.
3rd row P1, k1, p1, C4B, p1, k1, p1.
4th row P1, k1, p6, k1, p1.
These 4 rows form the patt and are repeated throughout.

BACK
With 3mm (No 11/US 2) needles, cast on 101(119) sts.
Beg with a k row, work 6 rows in st st for rolled edging, so ending
with a WS (purl) row.
P 4 rows, so ending with a WS row.
Beg and ending rows where indicated for chosen size, work 9
rows in patt from Chart, so ending with a RS row.
P 4 rows, so ending with a RS row.

Change to 3¼mm (No 10/US 3) needles.
Beg with a p row, work in st st until back measures 18(24)cm/
7(9½)in from cast-on edge, ending with a WS (purl) row.
P 4 rows, so ending with a WS row.
Work 9 rows in patt from Chart, so ending with a RS row.
P 4 rows, so ending with a RS row.
Inc across next row as foll:
Next row (WS) P18(17), [m1, p22(17)] 3(5) times, m1, p17.
105(125) sts.
1st size only
Next row (RS) Work 1st row of Panels A, B, C, B, A, D, C, D, A.
Next row Work 2nd row of Panels A, D, C, D, A, B, C, B, A.
2nd size only
Next row (RS) Work 1st row of Panels B, A, B, C, B, A, D, C, D,
A, D.

Next row Work 2nd row of Panels D, A, D, C, D, A, B, C, B, A, B.

Both sizes

These last 2 rows set the patt.**

Cont in patt as set until 84 rows have been worked in panel patts.

Shape Shoulders

Keeping patt correct as set and casting off in patt, cast off 32(40) sts at beg of next 2 rows. Cast off rem 41(45) sts.

FRONT

Work as given for back to **.

Cont in patt as set until 64 rows have been worked in panel patts, so ending with a WS row.

Shape Neck

Keeping patt correct as set throughout, divide for neck on next row as foll:

Next row (RS) Work 40(48) sts in patt, work 2 sts tog, then turn, leaving rem sts on a spare needle.

Working on this set of sts for first side of neck, dec one st at neck edge on every foll alt row until 32(40) sts rem.

Work one row without shaping, so ending with a WS row.

Cast off 32(40) sts.

With RS facing, rejoin yarn to rem sts, cast off first 21(25) sts for centre front neck, then work 2 sts tog, work in patt to end.

Complete to match first side.

SLEEVES (make 2)

With 3mm (No 11/US 2) needles, cast on 51(55) sts.

Beg with a k row, work 6 rows in st st for rolled edging, so ending with a WS (purl) row.

P 4 rows, so ending with a WS row.

Beg and ending rows where indicated for chosen sleeve size, work 9 rows in patt from Chart, so ending with a RS row.

P 4 rows, so ending with a RS row.

Change to 3¼mm (No 10/US 3) needles.

Beg with a p row, work in st st, inc one st at each end of the 2nd row and then every foll 4th row until there are 69(77) sts, so ending with a RS (knit) row.

P 4 rows, so ending with a RS row.

Inc across next row as foll:

Next row (WS) P2(6), [m1, p22] 3 times, m1, p1(5). 73(81) sts.

1st size only

Next row (RS) Work last 7 sts of 1st row of Panel B; work entire 1st row of Panels C, B, A, D, C; work first 7 sts of 1st row of Panel D.

Next row Work last 7 sts of 2nd row of Panel D; work entire 2nd row of Panels C, D, A, B, C; work first 7 sts of 2nd row of Panel B.

2nd size only

Next row (RS) Work last st of 1st row of Panel A; work entire 1st row of Panels B, C, B, A, D, C, D; work first st of 1st row of Panel A.

Next row Work last st of 2nd row of Panel A; work entire 2nd row of Panels D, C, D, A, B, C, B; work first st of 2nd row of Panel A.

Both sizes

These last 2 rows set the patt.

Cont in patt, inc one st at each end of the next row and then every foll 4th row until there are 91(99) sts, working extra sts into patt. Work in patt without shaping until 42 rows have been worked in panel patts.

Cast off in patt.

HOOD

With 3¼mm (No 10/US 3) needles, cast on 57(63) sts.

1st row K to end.

2nd row K5, p to end.

Rep last 2 rows until hood measures 51(55)cm/20(21¾)in ending with a WS row.

Cast off.

TO MAKE UP

Join shoulder seams. Sew on sleeves, matching centre of sleeve to shoulder seam. Join side and sleeve seams, reversing seam over st st section to roll back at hems.

Fold hood in half and join back seam. Sew hood in place, beginning and ending at centre of cast-off front neck sts.

The rolled edge on the sleeve cuff and lower welts is created by introducing a stocking stitch border which curls back. It is often used in traditional Guernsey patterns.

Cabled Sweater

This Aran-style sweater is worked in a pure wool Aran-weight yarn. Together with its series of interlocking cables, this makes it a real winter warmer.

MATERIALS

15 x 100g (3¹/₂oz) hanks of Rowan *Magpie Aran*
Pair each of 4mm (UK No 8/US size 6) and 4¹/₂mm (UK No 7/ US size 7) knitting needles
Cable needle

SIZE AND MEASUREMENTS

To fit bust		
	86–97cm	
	34–38in	

Finished knitted measurements

Around bust	120	cm
	47¹/₄	in
Length to shoulder	66	cm
	26	in
Sleeve length	43	cm
	17	in

TENSION

18 sts and 26 rows to 10cm/4in over st st using 4¹/₂mm (UK No 7/US size 7) needles.
Panel D measures 11cm/4¹/₂in across.

ABBREVIATIONS

T3F (twist 3 front) = slip next 2 sts onto a cable needle and leave at front of work, p1, then k2 from cable needle.
T3B (twist 3 back) = slip next st onto a cable needle and leave at back of work, k2, then p1 from cable needle.
C4F (cable 4 front) = slip next 2 sts onto a cable needle and leave at front of work, k2, then k2 from cable needle.
C4B (cable 4 back) = slip next 2 sts onto a cable needle and leave at back of work, k2, then k2 from cable needle.
See also page 21.

PANEL PATTERNS

The following are the panel patts used on the sweater:

Panel A (worked over 12 sts)
1st row (RS) K2, p2, k4, p2, k2.
2nd row P2, k2, p4, k2, p2.
3rd row K2, p2, C4F, p2, k2.
4th row As 2nd row.
These 4 rows form the patt and are repeated throughout.

Panel B (worked over 26 sts)
1st row (RS) P2, [T3F, T3B, p2] 3 times.
2nd row K3, [p4, k4] twice, k3.

3rd row P3, [C4F, p4] twice, C4F, p3.
4th row As 2nd row.
5th row P2, [T3B, T3F, p2] 3 times.
6th row K2, [p2, k2] 6 times.
7th–12th rows Rep 1st–6th rows once more.
13th row P1, [T3B, p2, T3F] 3 times, p1.
14th row K1, p2, [k4, p4] twice, k4, p2, k1.
15th row P1, k2, [p4, C4B] twice, p4, k2, p1.
16th row As 14th row.
17th row P1, k2, p3, [T3B, T3F, p2] twice, p1, k2, p1.
18th row K1, p2, k3, [p2, k2] 4 times, k1, p2, k1.
19th row P1, k2, p3, [T3F, T3B, p2] twice, p1, k2, p1.
20th row As 14th row.
21st row As 15th row.
22nd row As 14th row.
23rd row P1, [T3F, p2, T3B] 3 times, p1.
24th row K2, [p2, k2] 6 times.
These 24 rows form the patt and are repeated throughout.

Panel C (worked over 15 sts)
1st row (RS) P3, T3F, T3B, T3F, p3.
2nd row K3, p2, k2, p4, k4.
3rd row P4, C4B, p2, k2, p3.
4th row K3, p2, k2, p4, k4.
5th row P3, T3B, T3F, T3B, p3.
6th row K4, p4, k2, p2, k3.
7th row P3, k2, p2, C4F, p4.
8th row K4, p4, k2, p2, k3.
These 8 rows form the patt and are repeated throughout.

Panel D (worked over 32 sts)
1st row (RS) P7, [T3B, T3F] 3 times, p7.
2nd row K7, p2, k2, p4, k2, p4, k2, p2, k7.
3rd row P6, T3B, [p2, C4B] twice, p2, T3F, p6.
4th row and every foll even-numbered row K all the k sts and p the p sts.
5th row P5, T3B, p2, [T3B, T3F] twice, p2, T3F, p5.
7th row P4, [T3B, p2] twice, C4F, [p2, T3F] twice, p4.
9th row P3, [T3B, p2] twice, T3B, T3F, [p2, T3F] twice, p3.
11th row P3, [k2, p3] twice, k2, p2, k2, [p3, k2] twice, p3.
13th row P3, [T3F, p2] twice, T3F, T3B, [p2, T3B] twice, p3.
15th row P4, [T3F, p2] twice, C4F, [p2, T3B] twice, p4.
17th row P5, T3F, p2, [T3F, T3B] twice, p2, T3B, p5.
19th row P6, T3F, [p2, C4B] twice, p2, T3B, p6.
21st row P7, [T3F, T3B] 3 times, p7.
23rd row P8, [C4F, p2] twice, C4F, p8.
24th row K8, [p4, k2] twice, p4, k8.
These 24 rows form the patt and are repeated throughout.

BACK and FRONT (both alike)

With 4mm (No 8/US 6) needles, cast on 158 sts.
Beg cabled rib patt as foll:
1st rib row (RS) K2, [p2, k2] 11 times, p3, k2, p2, k2, p3, k2,

[p2, k2] 10 times, p3, k2, p2, k2, p3, [k2, p2] 11 times, k2.

2nd rib row Rib 4, m1, p2, m1, rib 34, m1, p2, m1, rib 20, m1, p2, m1, rib 30, m1, p2, m1, rib 20, m1, p2, m1, rib 34, m1, p2, m1, rib 4. 170 sts.

3rd rib row Work 3rd row of Panel A, rib 26, work 3rd row of Panel A, rib 12, work 3rd row of Panel A, rib 22, work 3rd row of Panel A, rib 12, work 3rd row of Panel A, rib 26, work 3rd row of Panel A.

4th rib row Work 4th row of Panel A, rib 26, work 4th row of Panel A, rib 12, work 4th row of Panel A, rib 22, work 4th row of Panel A, rib 12, work 4th row of Panel A, rib 26, work 4th row of Panel A.

Work 7 rows more in patt as set, so ending with a RS row.

Inc across next row as foll:

12th rib row (WS) Work 4th row of Panel A, rib 26, work 4th row of Panel A, m1, rib 3, m1, p2, m1, rib 7, work 4th row of Panel A, rib 2, [m1, rib 2] 10 times, work 4th row of Panel A, m1, rib 3, m1, p2, m1, rib 7, work 4th row of Panel A, rib 26, work 4th row of Panel A. 186 sts.

Change to 4½mm (No7/US 7) needles and beg main cable patt as foll:

1st patt row Work 1st row of Panels A, B, A, C, A, D, A, C, A, B, A.

2nd patt row Work 2nd row of Panels, A, B, A, C, A, D, A, C, A, B, A.

These last 2 rows set the patt.

Cont in patt as set until work measures about 62cm/24½in from cast-on edge, ending with an 8th row of Panels B and D.

Shape Neck

Keeping patt correct as set throughout, divide for neck on next row as foll:

Next row (RS) Work 65 sts in patt, then turn, leaving rem sts on a spare needle.

Working on this set of sts only for first side of neck, dec one st at neck edge on every foll alt row until 60 sts rem, ending with a RS row.

Next row (WS) P1, k1, p2tog twice, k4, p2, k2, p2tog twice, k2, p2 over Panels C and A; k1, p2, k4, p2tog twice, k4, p2tog twice, k4, p2, k1, over Panel B; p2, k2, p2tog twice, k2, p2 over Panel A. Cast off in patt.

Return to rem sts and with RS facing, slip centre 56 sts onto a st holder or spare needle, then rejoin yarn to rem sts and work in patt to end.

Dec one st at neck edge on every foll alt row until 60 sts rem, ending with a RS row.

Next row (WS) P2, k2, p2tog twice, k2, p2 over Panel A; k1, p2, k4, p2tog twice, k4, p2tog twice, k4, p2, k1 over Panel B; p2, k2, p2tog twice, k2, p2 over Panel A; k3, p2tog, k2, p2tog, p1 over rem Panel C.

Cast off in patt.

SLEEVES (make 2)

With 4mm (No 8/US 6) needles, cast on 66 sts.

Beg cabled rib patt as foll:

1st rib row (RS) P3, k2, p2, k2, p3, k2, [p2, k2] 10 times, p3, k2, p2, k2, p3.

2nd rib row Rib 16, m1, p2, m1, rib 30, m1, p2, m1, rib 16. 70 sts.

3rd rib row Rib 12, work 3rd row of Panel A, rib 22, work 3rd row of Panel A, rib 12.

4th rib row Rib 12, work 4th row of Panel A, rib 22, work 4th row of Panel A, rib 12.

Work 7 rows more in patt as set, so ending with a RS row.

Inc across next row as foll:

12th rib row (WS) Rib 1, m1, rib 2, m1, p2, m1, rib 7, work across 4th row of Panel A, rib 2, [m1, rib 2] 10 times, work across 4th row of Panel A, m1, rib 3, m1, p2, m1, rib 7. 86 sts.

Change to 4¹⁄₂mm (No7/US 7) needles and beg main cable patt as foll:

1st patt row (RS) Work 1st row of Panels, C, A, D, A, C.

2nd patt row Work 2nd row of Panels, C, A, D, A, C.

These last 2 rows set the patt.

Keeping patt correct as set throughout, inc one st at each end of next row and then every foll 4th and 3rd rows alternately until there are 138 sts, working extra sts into patt as foll: *on right-hand side of sleeve*, take first 12 sts into Panel A, next 10 sts into first 10 sts of Panel A, and rem 4 sts into rev st st; *on left-hand side of sleeve*, take first 12 sts into Panel A, next 10 sts into last 10 sts of Panel A, and rem 4 sts into rev st st.

Work without shaping until sleeve measures 43cm/17in from cast-on edge, ending with a WS row.

Cast off in patt.

COLLAR (back and front alike)

Using 4mm (No 8/US 6) needles and with RS facing, pick up and k 10 sts down left side of neck, work in patt across 56 sts from holder, pick up and k10 sts up right side of neck. 76 sts.

1st row (WS) P2, k2, p4, k2, work 56 sts in patt, k2, p4, k2, p2.

2nd row K2, p2, C4F, p2, work 56 sts in patt, p2, C4F, p2, k2.

3rd row P2, k2, p4, k2, work 56 sts in patt, k2, p4, k2, p2.

Work 11 rows more in patt as set.

15th row P2, k2, p2tog twice, k2, p2, k2, p2tog twice, k2, p2, k8, p2tog twice, k2, p2tog twice, k2, p2tog twice, k8, p2, k2, p2tog twice, k2, p2, k2, p2tog twice, k2, p2.

Cast off in patt.

TO MAKE UP

Join shoulder and neckband seams. Sew on sleeves, matching centre of sleeve to shoulder seam. Join side and sleeve seams.

The four-stitch cables on this sweater run down into the ribs to create interest in the borders. The stitch patterns are carried into the neckband to make it stand away from the neck.

Man's Denim Guernsey

This generous man's sweater is based on traditional Guernsey patterning. Knitted in a hardwearing, practical denim yarn, the garment will fade beautifully with washing and wearing.

MATERIALS

26(29) x 50g (1³/₄oz) balls of Rowan *Denim*
Pair each of 3¹/₄mm (UK No 10/US size 3) and 4mm (UK No 8/ US size 6) knitting needles
Cable needle

SIZES AND MEASUREMENTS

To fit chest	102–107	112–117	cm
	40–42	44–46	in
Finished knitted measurements (after washing)			
Around chest	140	152	cm
	55	60	in
Length to shoulder	70	70	cm
	27¹/₂	27¹/₂	in
Sleeve length	48	48	cm
	19	19	in

TENSION BEFORE WASHING

See basic information about denim yarn on page 11.
20 sts and 28 rows to 10cm/4in over st st using 4mm (UK No 8/US size 6) needles.

ABBREVIATIONS

C6F (cable 6 front) = slip next 3 sts onto a cable needle and leave at front of work, k3, then k3 from cable needle.
See also page 21.

PANEL PATTERNS

The following are the panel patts used on the Man's Denim Guernsey:

Panel A (worked over 16 sts)
1st row (RS) P2, k5, p2, k5, p2.
2nd row K2, p4, k4, p4, k2.
3rd row P2, k3, p1, k1, p2, k1, p1, k3, p2.
4th row K2, p2, k1, p2, k2, p2, k1, p2, k2.
5th row P2, k1, p1, k3, p2, k3, p1, k1, p2.
6th row K3, p4, k2, p4, k3.
These 6 rows form the patt and are repeated throughout.

Panel B (worked over 9 sts)
1st row (RS) K2, [p1, k1] twice, p1, k2.
2nd row P3, k1, p1, k1, p3.
These 2 rows form the patt and are repeated throughout.

Panel C (worked over 6 sts)
1st row (RS) K6.
2nd row P6.
3rd row C6F.
4th row P6.
5th and 6th rows As 1st and 2nd rows.
These 6 rows form the patt and are repeated throughout.

BACK and FRONT (both alike)

With 3¹/₄mm (No 10/US 3) needles, cast on 140(152) sts.
K 11 rows for garter st band.
Change to 4mm (No 8/US 6) needles and beg with a k row, work in st st until work measures 50cm/19³/₄in from cast-on edge, ending with a RS (knit) row.

Yoke pattern
Inc across next row to prepare for yoke patt as foll:
Next row (WS) P7(13), *m1, p14; rep from * to last 7(13) sts, m1, p7(13). 150(162) sts.

1st size only
Next row (RS) P1, work 1st row of Panels A, B, p2, work 1st row of Panels C, A, B, p2, work 1st row of Panels C, A, C, p2, work 1st row of Panels B, A, C, p2, work 1st row of Panels B, A, p1.
Next row K1, work 2nd row of Panels A, B, k2, work 2nd row of Panels C, A, B, k2, work 2nd row of Panels C, A, C, k2, work 2nd row of Panels B, A, C, k2, work 2nd row of Panels B, A, k1.

2nd size only
Next row (RS) P1, work 1st row of Panels C, A, B, p2, work 1st row of Panels C, A, B, p2, work 1st row of Panels C, A, C, p2, work 1st row of Panels B, A, C, p2, work 1st row of Panels B, A, C, p1.
Next row K1, work 2nd row of Panels C, A, B, k2, work 2nd row of Panels C, A, B, k2, work 2nd row of Panels C, A, C, k2, work 2nd row of Panels B, A, C, k2, work 2nd row of Panels B, A, C, k1.

Both sizes
These last 2 rows set the patt.
Cont in patt as set until work measures 82cm/32in from cast-on edge, ending with 6th row of Panels A and C.

Shape Neck
Keeping patt correct as set throughout, divide for neck shaping on next row as foll:
Next row (RS) Work 59(65) sts in patt, then turn, leaving rem sts on a spare needle.
Working on this set of sts only for first side of neck, dec one st at neck edge on every foll alt row until 55(61) sts rem.
Work 3 rows without shaping, ending with 6th row of Panels A and C at armhole edge.
Leave rem sts on a holder for shoulder.
With RS facing, slip centre 32 sts onto a holder for centre neck, then rejoin yarn to rem sts and work in patt to end.
Complete to match first side, but ending with 6th row of Panels A and C *at neck edge.*

SLEEVES (make 2)

With 3¹/₄mm (No 10/US 3) needles, cast on 62 sts.

Beg k2, p2 ribbing as foll:

1st rib row K2, *p2, k2; rep from * to end.

2nd rib row P2, *k2, p2; rep from * to end.

Rep last 2 rows 24 times more.

Change to 4mm (No 8/US 6) needles and beg with a k row, work in st st, inc one st at each end of the 5th row and then every foll 6th row until there are 88 sts, so ending with a RS row.

Work 2 rows without shaping, so ending with a RS row.

Next row (WS) P to end, inc 2 sts evenly across row. 90 sts.

Beg patt as foll:

Next row Work last 4 sts of 1st row of Panel C, work 1st row of Panels A and B, p2, work 1st row of Panels C, A, C, p2, work 1st row of Panels B and A, work first 4 sts of 1st row of Panel C.

Next row Work last 4 sts of 2nd row of Panel C, work 2nd row of Panels A and B, k2, work 2nd row of Panels C, A, C, k2, work 2nd row of Panels B and A, work first 4 sts of 2nd row of panel C.

These last 2 rows set the patt.

Cont in patt as set, inc one st at each end of the next row and every foll 8th row, and working extra sts into patt, until there are 102 sts.

Work in patt without shaping until sleeve measures 68cm/26³/₄in from cast-on edge, ending with a WS row.

Cast off in patt.

COLLAR

Join right shoulder seam.

Using 3¹/₄mm (No 10/US 3) needles and with RS facing, pick up and k 12 sts down left front neck, work in patt across 32 sts from centre front holder, pick up and k 12 sts up right front neck, 12 sts down right back neck, work in patt across 32 sts from centre back holder, pick up and k 12 sts up left back neck. 112 sts.

1st row (WS) Work 12 sts in moss st, work in patt as set across next 32 sts, work 24 sts in moss st, work in patt as set across next 32 sts, work 12 sts in moss st.

Work 16 rows more in patt as set.

Dec 2 sts over each cable, cast off in patt.

TO MAKE UP

Join left shoulder seam and neckband. Wash pieces according to yarn label and instructions for denim yarn on page 11.

Sew on sleeves, matching centre of sleeve to shoulder seam.

Leaving side vents open along garter st band, join side and sleeve seams, reversing seam for cuff foldback.

The neckband is worked in moss stitch, and cables carried up from the body. As the denim yarn fades on this Guernsey it will highlight the textured stitches.

Colour Knitting From earth tones to brights, from pastels to neutrals, colour – used on it's own or combined – breathes life into any handknit

Colour knitting basics

Colour knitting covers a range of techniques, and you will need to choose the one that suits the type of colour knitting you are working on. The three basic techniques are stranding yarns, weaving in yarns and intarsia knitting. If you want to learn the techniques from scratch or just brush up on them, follow the step-by-step instructions on these two pages. My special tips for colour knitting are given on pages 70–72.

Stranding

Stranding is used when colours are worked over a small amount of stitches, usually a maximum of four. The yarns are picked up over and under one another, which prevents them from tangling. It is the technique used for the small repeats in Fair Isle patterns where only two colours are used in a single row. All you have to do when 'stranding' is leave the colour you are not knitting with hanging on the wrong side of the knitting and pick it up again when you need it. This creates loose strands or 'floats' on the wrong side.

STRANDING ON A KNIT ROW

1 On a right-side (knit) row, to change colours drop the colour you were using. Then pick up the new colour, take it *over* the top of the dropped colour and start knitting with it.

2 To change back to the old colour, drop the colour you were knitting with. Then pick up the old colour, take it *under* the dropped colour and knit to the next colour change, and so on.

STRANDING ON A PURL ROW

1 On a wrong-side (purl) row, to change colours drop the colour you were using. Then pick up the new colour, take it *over* the top of the dropped colour and start purling with it.

2 To change back to the old colour, drop the colour you were knitting with. Then pick up the old colour, take it *under* the dropped colour and purl to the next colour change, and so on.

Weaving in

When there are more than four stitches between colour changes, long floats at the back of the work can make the knitted fabric too inflexible. These long floats can also catch on fingers, particularly on the inside of sleeves, which is especially inconvenient on children's garments. This is when the 'weaving in' technique, where the floats are caught into the back of the stitches, is used.

WEAVING IN ON A KNIT ROW

1 To weave yarn on a knit stitch, insert the right-hand needle into the next stitch and lay the yarn to be woven in over the right-hand needle. Knit the stitch with working yarn, taking it under the yarn not in use and making sure you do not catch this strand into the knitted stitch.

2 Knit the next stitch with the working yarn, taking it over the yarn being woven in. Continue like this, weaving the loose colour over and under the working yarn alternately with each stitch until you need to use it again.

WEAVING IN ON A PURL ROW

1 To weave yarn on a purl stitch, insert the right-hand needle into the next stitch and lay the yarn to be woven in over the right-hand needle. Purl the stitch with working yarn, taking it under the yarn not in use and making sure you do not catch this strand into the purled stitch.

2 Purl the next stitch with the working yarn, taking it over the yarn being woven in. Continue like this, weaving the loose colour over and under the working yarn alternately with each stitch until you need to use it again.

Working intarsia motifs

Intarsia is used when blocks of colour are being worked in separate areas of the knitted fabric. For these types of designs, there is no need to carry the colour (or colours) used for the motif across the entire row of knitting. Also, weaving in or stranding yarns would make the fabric too rigid, and it would look messy on the right side. By using a separate ball (or balls) of yarn for each area of colour and twisting the yarns together where they meet, the fabric will look neat and lie flat. This is called the 'intarsia' technique.

CHANGING COLOURS ON A VERTICAL LINE

If the two colour areas are forming a vertical line, to change colours on a knit row drop the colour you were using. Pick up the new colour and wrap it around the dropped colour as shown, then continue with the new colour. Twist the yarns together on knit and purl rows in this same way at vertical-line colour changes.

CHANGING COLOURS ON A RIGHT DIAGONAL

If the two colour areas are forming a right diagonal line, on a knit row drop the colour you were using. Pick up the new colour and wrap it around the dropped colour as shown, then continue with the new colour. Twist the yarns together on knit rows only at right-diagonal colour changes.

CHANGING COLOURS ON A LEFT DIAGONAL

If the two colour areas are forming a left diagonal line, on a purl row drop the colour you were using. Pick up the new colour and wrap it around the colour you just dropped as shown, then continue with the new colour. Twist the yarns together on purl rows only at left-diagonal colour changes.

Working from a chart

Colour designs for knitting are usually given as a chart on a squared graph. Each square on the chart represents a stitch and each horizontal row of squares represents a row of knitting. The colours are shown on the chart either as actual colours or as symbols. Just as you knit starting at the bottom of your knitting and working upwards, so you read the chart – from the bottom row upwards to the top row. Unless stated otherwise, the first row of the knitting chart represents the first row of the knitting, and it is followed from right to left and worked in knit stitches. The second row of the chart represents the second row of knitting, which is a purl row, and it is read from left to right.

If the colour pattern is a repeated design, the chart will indicate how many stitches are in each repeat. The stitches before and after the repeat are the 'edge stitches'. You knit the edge stitches at the beginning of the row, then knit the 'repeat' as many times as necessary until you reach the edge stitches at the end of the row.

The number of rows in the pattern repeat is usually as many rows as there are on the chart.

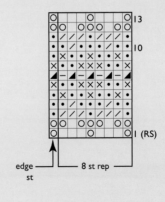

edge st — 8 st rep

Key

- ☐ main colour (A)
- ⊙ Pale Blue
- • Cream
- ⧸ Dark Blue
- ✕ Lilac
- ◢ Dark Red
- — Pale Yellow

Stranding and weaving-in class

Knitting these three simple swatches is the best lesson I can think of for learning the stranding and weaving-in colourwork techniques and for discovering how to work new colour combinations.

Colour knitting is simple

Many knitters are put off by colour knitting because they think it is more difficult than it really is. One or two bad experiences mean that they avoid it in the future, because they feel they are not proficient enough to tackle it. In reality, colour knitting is simple as long as you know what technique is appropriate for a particular type of colourwork.

Making colour swatches

Making the swatches pictured here and on the following two pages will take you through all the colour techniques that you will need to know – stranding, weaving in and intarsia. My swatches were knitted in a good-quality cotton, but you may feel that for your first attempts wool – being a more 'forgiving' yarn with fibres that draw the stitches together – would suit you best. If you do use cotton, remember that poor-quality, or stringy, cotton can make colourwork look less tidy than when worked in a better-quality one.

I like to work a border of garter stitch or moss stitch around my colour samples. It makes them look neater, and if you have a border, you don't have to sew in the yarn ends at the selvedges.

Stranding yarns

The stranding technique is used when each colour is only used over a few – usually less than four – stitches. To practice stranding, try knitting a simple checkerboard pattern. First, cast on a multiple of stitches divisible by three, plus any stitches you wish

to work as your border on either side. Before starting the colour pattern, work your lower border in a single colour. Then on the first colourwork row, work three stitches in your contrast colour and three stitches in your main colour alternately along the row, using the techniques shown on page 68 to avoid twisting and tangling your yarns. Work four rows like this, then alternate the colours to create the checkerboard effect.

Try to make sure that you are feeling fairly relaxed – anxiety is bound to make your knitting tighter! Your aim is to keep your knitting relaxed so that you do not pull the yarn too tightly across the back of the work. Keep a good even tension and smooth your stitches out on the needle; if you do this, your colour knitting will lie as flat as stocking stitch in a single colour and will have the same amount of give. To make the exercise less monotonous, use other contrast colours on your pattern. I like to pat and 'tweak' my knitting when working in colour. Handling the knitted fabric can sometimes smooth out small inconsistencies, and you will be able to tell if your knitting is becoming too tight by how the stitches slip along the needle. If you haven't used them already, try bamboo needles – their silky finish makes them perfect for colour knitting.

A checkerboard is a useful colour design to master. It can look good as a gingham, with one contrast shade a deeper tone than the other. Checks work really well when contrasted with other patterns such as florals or Fair Isles.

On completion of your swatch, press it lightly and check to make sure that the fabric has not pulled in over the colourwork.

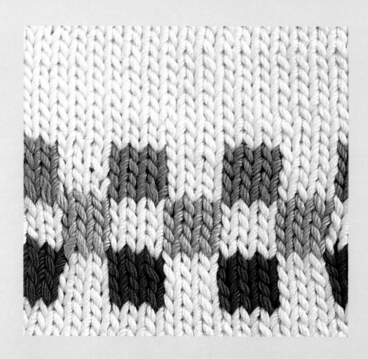

Weaving in yarns

The weaving-in technique is used when a single colour is worked over more than four stitches. Without weaving in you would have long floats on the wrong side of the knitting that not only create a rigid, inflexible fabric, but also catch on fingers and watches, etc. This can be a particular nightmare on babywear as you try and negotiate small fingers down sleeves!

For your weaving-in swatch, cast on a multiple of six stitches plus one extra, plus your border stitches. On your first colour row, work one stitch in the contrast colour and five stitches in the main colour alternately along the row. Weave in on the middle stitch in the main shade between the stitches in the contrast colour using the technique shown on page 69. Continue to work the chevron pattern as shown on the swatch below.

This small chevron pattern is ideal for practising this technique, as you only need to weave in on the first row (a right-side row) and the last row (a wrong-side row). This demonstrates that often on Fair Isles you only need to use the technique as and when required. Don't weave in on alternate stitches, as this makes the fabric too rigid, and the contrast colour will show through. In some small Fair Isle patterns you may only need to use stranding, in others a combination of stranding and weaving in.

Combining colours

The Fair Isle swatch below is a good example of how effective the simplest of Fair Isles can be. Any Fair Isle, however small, has enormous possibilities. Choose a colour pattern from a Fair Isle chart and see how many variations you can achieve. By using a thicker weight yarn, or using bold colours on a dark background and pastel shades on a light background, you can see the endless variations that you can get out of just one pattern.

It can also demonstrate just how hard working with colour can be. Shades that look wonderful in the ball before you start knitting can look disappointing when knitted up. This is often due to the proportion you use of each colour. A strong shade can overpower a softer one, or a subtle dusky shade can look dirty when put against a brighter one. It sometimes takes me four or five attempts before I find a colourway that I am happy with. If there are one or two rows that you feel don't work, try Swiss darning over them in other colours to see if they work better (see page 87).

WEAVING-IN TIP
If you are weaving in a yarn on the wrong side of your knitting, it is best to avoid any very strong contrasts in colour, as the woven-in yarn may show through to the other side. It looks particularly unattractive when a very dark shade can be seen behind the stitches of a far lighter shade.

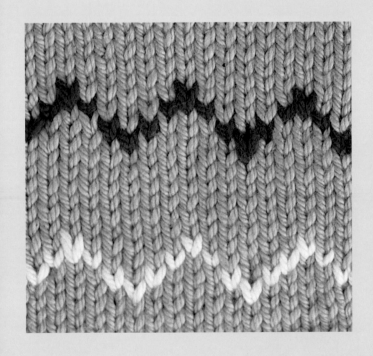

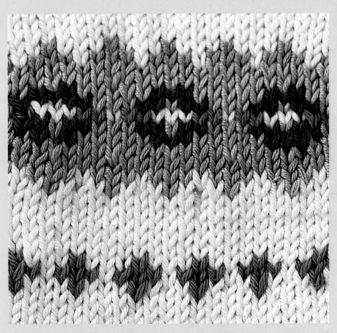

Intarsia class

In intarsia knitting the yarn colours are not carried across the back of the fabric as for stranding or weaving in. Instead the yarns are kept only in the area of the individual motifs. Try these exercises to practise and perfect the technique.

Practising a vertical colour change

The intarsia technique is used when individual blocks of colour are worked. This can mean that on some motif knitting you may have to work with a lot of separate lengths of yarn across a row. Do not be tempted to avoid this by using the stranding or weaving-in techniques – your motifs won't lie flat, and the main background colour may well show through.

The best way to try out intarsia is to knit a swatch where two colours are divided vertically, using the techniques on page 69, which show how to twist the main colour and contrast colour to avoid holes. It will allow you to practice twisting yarns until you achieve the neatest possible effect. You will notice that there is a slight difference in size between the stitch at the colour change in one row and the one above. It is very difficult to achieve the perfect match, but you can make the colour change as even as possible by trying to ensure that you knit the wrong-side rows at the same tension as right-side rows. At its worst, the looser stitch will bulge out as it is squeezed by the tighter stitch on the row above and below. Some discrepancies, you will be pleased to know, will often even out when the piece is washed or pressed!

Working repeated intarsia motifs

The floral swatch at the right is an example of using small amounts of separate strands of colour when working small motifs. Afterwards, these ends are darned in on the back, following the lines of the colour change so they do not show through to the other side.

Choosing colours for intarsia knitting

The floral motif would look equally good worked using rich colours against a dark background, or using tones of one colour, such as dark and light blues for the flower and leaves. There are fantastic colour ranges available from the spinners now. It can sometimes be as overwhelming as it is exciting when confronted in a yarn store by all the possibilities that are available to you. I find it helpful to keep a file of favourite postcards, images torn from magazines and printed fabrics that all have interesting colourways that I would not have necessarily come up with myself. They can often provide stimulus to creating your own colour combinations.

INTARSIA TIP
Try using medium lengths of yarn for each colour in your intarsia rather than using bobbins or small balls. The yarns are bound to tangle, and lengths of yarn can be pulled through if the colours do twist together.

TEST SWATCH TIP
Keep your test swatches, even if you feel they don't work because they are often useful for reference later on – if only to remind yourself not to go down that particular colour route again!

Fair Isle Socks

Handknitted socks are becoming more popular. The colour chart shows one version (the sock on the left), but try experimenting with other colour combinations with oddments of yarn.

MATERIALS

1 x 50g (1³/₄oz) ball of Jaeger *Baby Merino 4-ply* in main colour (A) and small amount in each of 6 contrast colours

Pair each of 2³/₄mm (UK No 12/US size 2) and 3¹/₄mm (UK No 10/US size 3) knitting needles

Set of four 3¹/₄mm (UK No 10/US size 3) double-pointed knitting needles

SIZE

To fit 13cm/5in foot length

TENSION

28 sts and 36 rows to 10cm/4in over st st on 3¹/₄mm (UK No 10/US size 3) needles.

ABBREVIATIONS

See page 21.

SPECIAL CHART NOTE

Read the chart from right to left on RS (odd-numbered) rows and from left to right on WS (even-numbered) rows. When working in colour patt, strand yarn not in use loosely across WS of work to keep fabric elastic.

TO MAKE

With 2³/₄mm (No 12/US 2) needles and yarn A, cast on 49 sts for cuff.

1st rib row K1, *p1, k1; rep from * to end.

2nd rib row P1, *k1, p1; rep from * to end.

Rep first row once more.

Change to 3¹/₄mm (No 10/US 3) needles and p one row.

Beg with a k row and working in st st, work first to 13th rows from Chart for colour patt, dec 6 sts evenly across 13th row. 43 sts.

Change to 2³/₄mm (No 12/US 2) needles.

Cont in yarn A only, work in rib until sock measures 12cm/4³/₄in from cast-on edge, ending with a RS row.

Change to 3¹/₄mm (No 10/US 3) needles.

Beg with a k row, work 4 rows st st.

Break off yarn.

With set of four 3¹/₄mm (No 10/US 3) double-pointed needles, divide sts onto 3 needles as foll: slip first 9 sts onto first needle, next 12 sts onto 2nd needle and next 12 sts onto 3rd needle, then slip last 10 sts onto other end of first needle.

Shape Heel

With RS facing, join yarn A to 19 sts on first needle, k9, k2tog, k8, turn.

Working on these 18 sts only, beg with a p row and work 9 rows st st, so ending with a WS (purl) row.

Next row K13, k2tog tbl, turn.

Next row Sl 1, p8, p2tog, turn.

**Next row Sl 1, k8, k2tog tbl, turn.

Next row Sl 1, p8, p2tog, turn.**

Rep from ** to ** twice. 10 sts.

Break off yarn.

Reset sts on 3 needles as foll: slip first 5 sts of heel sts onto a safety-pin, place marker here to indicate beg of round, join yarn A to rem sts, with first needle k5, then pick up and k 8 sts along side of heel, k5, with 2nd needle k14, with 3rd needle k5, then pick up and k 8 sts along other side of heel, k5 from safety-pin. 50 sts.

K one round

Next round K12, k2tog, k to last 14 sts, k2tog tbl, k12.

K one round.

Next round K11, k2tog, k to last 13 sts, k2tog tbl, k11.

Cont in this way, dec one st at each side of heel on every alt round until 40 sts rem.

Cont without shaping until sock measures 11cm/4¹/₄in from back of heel.

Shape Toe

Next round [K7, k2tog, k2, k2tog tbl, k7] twice.

K one round.

Next round [K6, k2tog, k2, k2tog tbl, k6] twice.

Cont in this way, dec 4 sts on every alt round until 20 sts rem.

Divide sts onto 2 needles – sole and instep – and graft sts tog.

Join back seam, reversing seam for turning.

Work second sock to match.

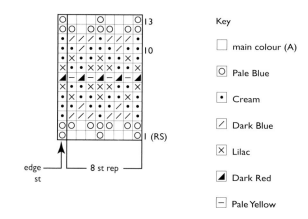

Key

☐ main colour (A)

◯ Pale Blue

• Cream

╱ Dark Blue

✕ Lilac

◢ Dark Red

— Pale Yellow

Child's Fair Isle Sweater

This classic, Fair Isle sweater has a 1940's retro feel, and is knitted in a soft, botany wool. The stranding technique is used for the Fair Isle patterning.

MATERIALS

2(2:2:2) x 50g (1³/₄oz) balls Rowan *True 4-ply Botany* in main colour (A), and 1 ball each in Navy, Pale Aqua, Cream, Pink, Dark Red and Yellow

Pair each of 2³/₄mm (UK No 12/US size 2) and 3¹/₄mm (UK No 10/US size 3) knitting needles

3 buttons

SIZES AND MEASUREMENTS

To fit ages	6–12	12–18	24–36	36–48 months
Finished knitted measurements				
Around chest	52	58	68	73	cm
	20¹/₂	22³/₄	26³/₄	28³/₄	in
Length to shoulder	23	28	34	38	cm
	9	11	13¹/₂	15	in
Sleeve length	8	10	12	14	cm
	3¹/₄	4	4³/₄	5¹/₂	in

TENSION

31 sts and 35 rows to 10cm/4in over st st on 3¹/₄mm (UK No 10/US size 3) needles.

ABBREVIATIONS

See page 21.

SPECIAL CHART NOTE

Read the chart from right to left on RS (odd-numbered) rows and from left to right on WS (even-numbered) rows. When working in colour patt, strand yarn not in use loosely across WS of work to keep fabric elastic.

BACK

With 2³/₄mm (No 12/US 2) needles and yarn A, cast on 82(90:106:114) sts.

1st rib row *K1, p1; rep from * to end.

Rep last row 7(9:11:13) times more, inc one st at centre of last row. 83(91:107:115) sts.

Change to 3¹/₄mm (No 10/US 3) needles and work 2 rows in st st.

Cont in st st and colour patt from Chart until back measures 13(16:20:22)cm/5(6¹/₄:7³/₄:8³/₄)in from cast-on edge, ending with a WS (purl) row.

Shape Armholes

Cont in patt from Chart throughout, cast off 4(5:7:8) sts at beg of next 2 rows.

Dec one st at armhole edge on next row and 3 foll alt rows.

67(73:85:91) sts.

Work without shaping until back measures 18(23:28:32)cm/7(9: 11:12¹/₂)in from cast-on edge, ending with a WS row.

Back Neck Opening

Divide for neck opening on next row as foll:

Next row (RS) K31(34:40:43), then turn, leaving rem sts on a spare needle.

Working on this set of sts only for first side of neck, work without shaping until back measures 23(28:34:38)cm/9(11:13¹/₂:15)in from cast-on edge, ending with a WS row.

Shape Shoulder

Cast off 10(11:13:14) sts at beg of next row and foll alt row.

Leave rem 11(12:14:15) sts on a holder.

With RS facing, slip centre 5 sts onto a safety pin, rejoin yarn to rem sts, then k to end. 31(34:40:43) sts.

Complete to match first side.

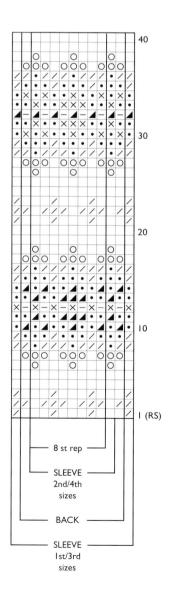

Key

- ☐ main colour (A)
- ╱ Navy
- ○ Pale Aqua
- • Cream
- ◢ Pink
- ✕ Dark Red
- ─ Yellow

A small buttoned back opening for a child's design ensures that the neckband fits snugly but can be easily pulled over the head.

FRONT

Work as given for back until front measures 18(23:28:32)cm/7(9: 11:12¹/₂)in from cast-on edge, ending with a WS row.

Neck Shaping

Divide for neck shaping on next row as foll:

Next row (RS) Work 25(27:32:34) sts in patt, then turn, leaving rem sts on a spare needle.

Working on this set of sts only for first side of neck, dec one st at neck edge on next row and every foll alt row until 20(22:26:28) sts rem.

Work without shaping until front matches back to shoulder shaping, ending with a WS row.

Shape Shoulders

Cast off 10(11:13:14) sts at beg of next row.

Work one row without shaping.

Cast off rem 10(11:13:14) sts.

With RS facing, slip centre 17(19:21:23) sts onto a st holder, rejoin yarn to rem sts, then work in patt to end.

Complete to match first side.

SLEEVES (make 2)

With 2³/₄mm (No 12/US 2) needles and yarn A, cast on 52(56:60:64) sts.

1st rib row (RS) *K1, p1; rep from * to end.

Rep last row 3(5:7:9) times more, inc one st at centre of last row. 53(57:61:65) sts.

Change to 3¹/₄mm (No 10/US 3) needles and work 2 rows in st st.

Cont in st st and colour patt from Chart **and at the same time** inc one st at each end of every foll 3rd row, working extra sts into patt, until there are 67(73:79:85) sts.

Cont in patt throughout, work without shaping until sleeve measures 8(10:12:14)cm/ 3¹/₄(4:4³/₄:5¹/₂)in from cast-on edge, ending with a WS row.

Shape Sleeve Top

Mark each end of last row with a coloured thread.

Work 4(6:8:10) rows more without shaping.

Dec one st at each end of next row and 3 foll alt rows. 59(65:71:77) sts.

Work one row without shaping.

Cast off.

BUTTON BAND

With 2³/₄mm (No 12/US 2) needles and yarn A, cast on 7 sts.

1st rib row (RS) P1, [k1, p1] twice, k2.

2nd rib row K1, * p1, k1; rep from * to end.

Cont in rib until band fits up right back neck opening to neck edge, ending with a WS row.

Break off yarn and leave sts on safety-pin.

Mark positions of buttons on button band, the first one 1.5cm/¹/₂in above lower edge, the last to come 1cm/³/₈in above neck edge (in neckband), and the rem button spaced evenly between these two.

BUTTONHOLE BAND

Using 2³/₄mm (No 12/US 2) needles and yarn A and with RS facing, join yarn to sts on safety-pin at centre of back neck opening, k3, m1, k2, then cast on one st at end of row. 7 sts.

1st rib row (WS) K1, * p1, k1; rep from * to end.

2nd rib row K2, p1, [k1, p1] twice.

Cont in rib until band fits up left back to neck shaping, ending with a WS row and **at the same time work** the first and 2nd buttonhole when reached as foll:

Buttonhole row (RS) Work 3 sts in rib, yf, rib 2 tog, work 2 sts in rib. Do not break off yarn at end of band.

NECKBAND

Join shoulder seams.

Using 2³/₄mm (No 12/US 2) needles and A and with RS facing, work 6 sts in rib from buttonhole band, rib next st tog with first st on back neck, k rem 10(11:13:14) sts, pick up and k12(14:16: 18) sts down left front neck, k across 17(19:21:23) sts of front neck, pick up and k 12(14:16:18) sts up right front neck, k across 10(11:13:14) sts from back neck, k next st tog with first st of button band, work rem 6 sts in rib. 75(83:93:101) sts.

Work 2cm/³/₄in in rib as set, working buttonhole at centre.

Cast off in rib.

TO MAKE UP

Sew on sleeve, sewing last 4(6:8:10) rows of straight sleeve edges (the section above markers) to the cast-off sts at underarm. Join side and sleeve seams. Stitch base of button band behind buttonhole band. Sew on buttons.

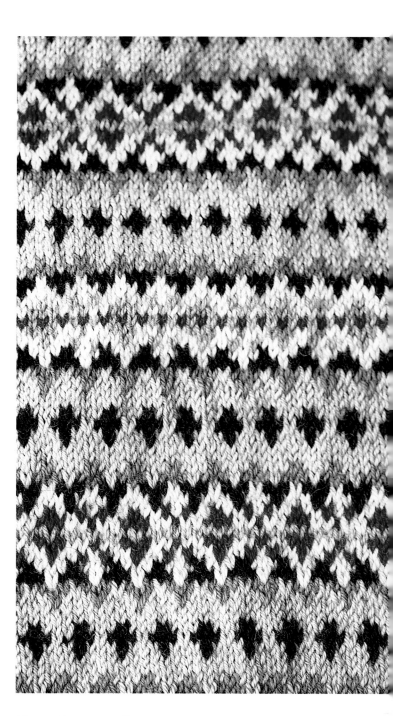

You could try some different colour combinations on this Fair Isle with some oddments of yarn. Use a different background colour or reverse the dark and light shades.

Floral Cardigan with Picot Edge

This slightly fitted cardigan combines a small rosebud pattern with a delicate picot edge. The intarsia method is used to work the delicate colour motifs.

MATERIALS

12(13:14) x 50g (1³⁄₄oz) balls of Rowan *Cotton Glacé* in main colour (M – Grey), 2 balls each in Dark Pink, Light Pink and Dark Green, and 1 ball in White
Pair of 3¹⁄₄mm (UK No 10/US size 3) knitting needles
9 buttons

SIZES AND MEASUREMENTS

To fit bust	86	92	97	cm
	34	36	38	in

Finished knitted measurements

Around bust	96	102	108	cm
	37³⁄₄	40	42¹⁄₂	in

Length to shoulder

	54	56	58	cm
	21¹⁄₄	22	22³⁄₄	in

Sleeve length	43	44	45	cm
	17	17¹⁄₂	17³⁄₄	in

TENSION

25 sts and 36 rows to 10cm/4in over patt using 3¹⁄₄mm (UK No 10/US size 3) needles.

ABBREVIATIONS

See page 21.

SPECIAL CHART NOTE

Read the chart from right to left on RS (odd-numbered) rows and from left to right on WS (even-numbered) rows. When working colour motifs, use separate lengths of contrasting colour for each coloured area and twist yarns together on WS at joins to avoid holes.

BACK

With 3¹⁄₄mm (No 10/US 3) needles and yarn M, cast on 122(130:138) sts.
Beg and ending rows where indicated for chosen size, work in patt from Chart for 24 rows.
Cont in patt from Chart throughout, dec one st at each end of next row and then every foll 6th row until 108(116:124) sts rem.
Work without shaping until back measures 21(22:23)cm/8¹⁄₄ (8¹⁄₂:9)in from cast-on edge, ending with a WS row.
Inc one st at each end of next row and then every foll 4th row until there are 122(130:138) sts.

Work without shaping until back measures 37(38:39)cm/14¹⁄₂ (15:15¹⁄₄)in from cast-on edge, ending with a WS row.

Shape Armholes

Cast off 8(9:10) sts at beg of next 2 rows.
Dec one st at each end of next row and then every foll alt row until 96(100:104) sts rem.
Work without shaping until back measures 54(56:58)cm/21¹⁄₄ (22:22³⁄₄)in from cast-on edge, ending with a WS row.

Shape Neck and Shoulders

Divide for neck shaping on next row as foll:
Next row (RS) Work 32(34:36) sts in patt, then turn, leaving rem sts on a spare needle.
Working on this set of sts only for first side of neck, cast off 3 sts at beg of next row, 9(10:11) sts at beg of next row, 2 sts at beg of next row and 9(10:11) sts at beg of next row.
Work one row without shaping.
Cast off rem 9 sts.
With RS facing, rejoin yarn to rem sts and cast off 32 sts for centre back neck, then work in patt to end. 32(34:36) sts.
Complete to match first side.

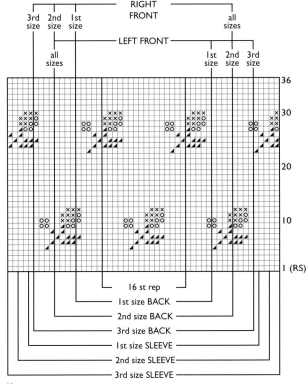

Key

☐ Grey (M)
◣ Dark Green
O Light Pink
✕ Dark Pink

LEFT FRONT

With 3¼mm (No 10/US 3) needles and yarn M, cast on 62(66: 70) sts.

Beg and ending rows where indicated for chosen size, work in patt from Chart for 24 rows.

Cont in patt from Chart throughout, dec one st at side edge on next row and then every foll 6th row until 55(59:63) sts rem.

Work without shaping until front measures 21(22:23)cm/8¼(8¼: 9)in from cast-on edge, ending with a WS row.

Inc one st at side edge on next row and then every foll 4th row until there are 62(66:70) sts.

Work without shaping until front measures 37(38:39)cm/14½ (15:15¼)in from cast-on edge, ending with a WS row.

Shape Armhole

Cast off 8(9:10) sts at beg of next row.

Work one row without shaping.

Dec one st at armhole edge on next row and then every foll alt row until 49(51:53) sts rem.

Shape Neck

Dec one st at neck edge on next row and every foll alt row until 31(33:35) sts rem, then on every foll 3rd row until 27(29:31) sts rem.

Work without shaping until front matches back to shoulder shaping, ending at armhole edge.

Shape Shoulder

Cast off 9(10:11) sts at beg of next row and then foll alt row.

Work one row without shaping.

Cast off rem 9 sts.

RIGHT FRONT

Work to match left front, reversing shaping.

SLEEVES (make 2)

With 3¼mm (No 10/US 3) needles and yarn M, cast on 44(48: 52) sts.

Beg and ending rows where indicated for chosen sleeve size, work in patt from Chart **and at the same time** inc one st at each end of the 3rd row and then every foll 8th row until there are 80(84:88) sts, working extra sts into patt.

Working in patt from Chart throughout, work without shaping until sleeve measures 43(44:45)cm/17(17½:17¾)in from cast-on edge, ending with a WS (purl) row.

Shape Sleeve Top

Mark each end of last row with a coloured thread.

Work 4(4:6) rows without shaping.

Dec one st at each end of next row and then every foll alt row until there are 70(72:74) sts.

Work one row without shaping.

Cast off 7 sts at beg of next 8 rows.

Cast off rem 14(16:18) sts.

BUTTONHOLE BAND

Using 3¼mm (No 10/US 3) needles and yarn M and with RS facing, beg at lower edge of right front and pick up and k 93(95:97) sts along front edge to beg of neck shaping.

K one row.

Next row (buttonhole row) (RS) K1(2:3), [k2tog, yf, k9] 8 times, k2tog, yf, k2(3:4).

K one row.

Cast off.

BUTTON BAND

Using 3¼mm (No 10/US 3) needles and yarn M and with RS facing, beg at neck shaping on left front and pick up and k 93(95:97) sts along front edge to cast-on edge.

K 3 rows.

Cast off.

SLEEVE EDGING

Using 3¼mm (No 10/US 3) needles and yarn M and with RS facing, pick up and k 45(49:53) sts along cast-on edge.

K one row.

Break off yarn M, and join on White.

Cast-off row (RS) Cast off 1 st knitwise, *slip st used in casting off back onto left-hand needle, cast on 2 sts knitwise, cast off 6 sts knitwise; rep from * to end. Fasten off.

TO MAKE UP

Join shoulder seams. Sew on sleeves, matching centre of sleeve to shoulder seam and sewing last 4(4:6) rows of side of sleeve to cast-off sts at underarm. Join side and sleeve seams.

Sew on buttons.

LOWER EDGING

Using 3¼mm (No 10/US 3) needles and yarn M and with RS facing, pick up and k 245(261:277) sts along cast-on edge of fronts and back, and edges of front bands.

Work as given for sleeve edging.

NECK EDGING

Using 3¼mm (No 10/US 3) needles and yarn M and with RS facing, pick up and k 65 sts across buttonhole band and up right front neck, 51 sts around back neck, 65 sts down left front neck and across button band. 181 sts.

Work as given for sleeve edging.

I used a chalky white to contrast sharply against the delicate floral motif. For a more subtle effect, you could work the pretty picot border in the main shade.

Embroidery on Knitting Enhance your handknits –
add a touch of texture or a dash of colour with surface embellishment

Embroidery basics

The knitted fabric is a good base for embroidery, as you can use the vertical and horizontal lines as a guide for where to put your stitches. I have included stitches here that I think look especially good on knitting

Starting the embroidery

Make sure that you choose your embroidery yarn or thread with care – too thin and it will disappear in the fabric, too thick and it will pull and distort the piece of knitting. Use a blunt-ended yarn or tapestry needle. Simple motifs or Swiss darning can be worked directly onto the knitting. For more intricate embroidery, the pattern can be drawn onto tissue paper, and then embroidered through the paper and the knitted fabric. The tissue can then be pulled away after the embroidery has been completed. When you start you embroidery, secure the end of the thread on the wrong side of the knitting before beginning the stitch or leave a long loose end to darn in later.

Cross stitch

Use the line of the knitted fabric as a guide by working over one, two or more knitted stitches and rows. Bring the needle and the thread through and make a diagonal stitch up and to the left. Make a row of diagonal stitches like this from right to left. Then make a return row of diagonal stitches completing the crosses from left to right as shown above.

Stem stitch

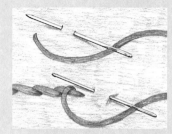

Bring the needle and the thread through the knitting, then insert the needle as shown, at a slight angle. Pull the needle through. Continue making short, slightly angled stitches in this way from left to right.

French knots

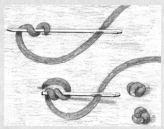

Bring needle and thread through, then wind the thread around the needle twice. Keeping the thread tautly wrapped around the needle, reinsert the needle very near where the thread first emerged and take it through to the back of the knitting. Bring the needle up in the correct position for the next knot.

Blanket stitch

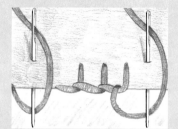

Secure the thread at the edge of the knitting. Insert the needle from front to back through the knitting a short distance from the edge and bring it out below the edge and with the thread under the needle point. Pull the thread through, then insert the needle in the same way, leaving a small gap between the stitches and bringing the needle out again below the edge and with the thread under the needle point. Continue like this along the edge.

Satin stitch

Swiss darning or duplicate stitch

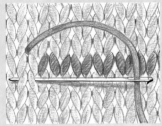

Bring the needle and thread through. Then work parallel stitches close together. The stitches can be made straight across or at an angle depending on the effect desired. Do not pull the thread too tightly or the knitting will become distorted.

1 Thread a blunt-ended needle with yarn the same weight as the stitch you are darning over. Bring the needle out at the base of the first stitch you want to cover, then take it under the base of the stitch above.

2 Take the needle back through the base of the first stitch and out at the base of the next stitch.
Cover each stitch this way.

Embroidery class

If colourwork knitting seems a bit daunting, try adding colour to a simple knit with embroidery. Some stitch techniques are given on pages 86 and 87, and here are some suggestions on how to use them on knitting and where to find inspiration.

Enhancing your knitwear

Embroidery is one of my favourite ways of enhancing my knitwear. A simple jacket can be transformed by using it on a collar or pocket. It can brighten up a dull garment or update a classic. I particularly love embroidery when it is used against a very contrasting yarn, brights worked on a rustic tweedy yarn or on the faded washed out blue of a denim (see Embroidered Denim Jacket on page 95).

Embroidering your knitting can also be a good way of adding colour to a garment if you are a fairly novice knitter and do not feel quite ready to tackle large areas of colourwork. On one of my first handknits, I worked tiny embroidered bees on the collar and cuffs of a simple white baby's cardigan – they provided surprisingly effective details.

Embroidery can also be used within the knitted stitch patterns. I have a cupboard full of old 1940's and 1950's knitting patterns that often include variations on Tyrolean designs where embroidery is used within the cable patterns. On the swatch below, I have used a simple cross stitch within a subtle Fair Isle pattern in duck egg blue, cream and a soft brown.

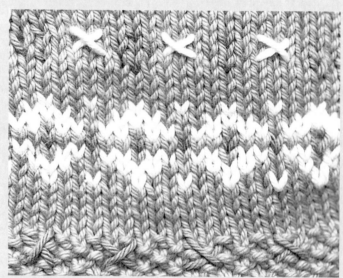

Finding inspiration for embroidery

I can be inspired by embroidery details on old fabrics found in junk shops and car boot or garage sales. A recent trip to Chinatown resulted in me staggering back home with a treasure trove of goodies – embroidered slippers and bags, and a tiny pair of silk shoes for a baby. I am lucky enough to live in a multi-ethnic part of London, where I am often dazzled by the wonderful fabrics on display in the local sari shops.

Embroidery on knitting can also be in the form of Swiss darning or duplicate stitch, which traces the path of the knit stitches. Influenced by American quilts and seventeenth-century samplers, I have designed knits where I have combined a patchwork of colour and texture. To prevent the colour being swamped by the texture, I have used Swiss darning to provide the colour rather than knitting it in, as it enhances the effect.

On a recent trip to America, I was privileged to be invited to see around the textile department of the Plymouth Plantation, a re-creation of one of the first European settlements on the East Coast. The department goes to great lengths to maintain authenticity in their costumes for the actors in their pageants, and I was thrilled to see delicate embroidery in progress on a child's knitted cap.

Translating inspiration into original design

My Child's Smock design on page 91 sprung from my interest in the history of workwear in England. I have always been particularly fascinated by the traditional farmers smock. My grandmother told me she remembered farmers wearing them to chapel in the 1920's – their wealth and status shown by the amount of embroidery worked on their smocks. The detailing on my knitted smock echoes that of the originals, with patterned yoke and sleeve and square collar. I am sure you will be pleased to see that rather than gathering the knitted fabric in, a false smocking is created by using a simple embroidery stitch on top of a diamond pattern.

Influenced by the stunning embroidery of my Hungarian Romany relations, I attempted more elaborate embroidery on the stocking stitch bolero pictured on page 95, trying to capture a folkloric, peasant look (see below right). The beauty of this style is that anyone can attempt it. Your embroidery stitches do not have to be perfectly applied. In fact, I think there can be an energy and charm in something that looks homemade in the best sense of the word. It looks more personal and less mass produced.

A special embroidered bag

The last project in this chapter is very special to me. One of my closest friends, a brilliant American knitwear designer called Pam Allen, was staying with me recently and held an embellishments class in my shop. We sat awestruck as she showed us swatch after swatch of the most exquisite embroidery on knitting. After that, I simply could not contemplate having a section in my book that did not include her truly inspirational work. I was delighted when she agreed to design the Embroidered Bag on page 101 especially for you.

Child's Smock

Based on a traditional nineteenth-century English farmers' smock, this knitwear design has soft gathers at the yoke, creating a pretty 'A'-line shape.

MATERIALS

8(9:10) x 50g (1³⁄₄oz) balls Jaeger *Pure Cotton* in main colour and one ball in contrast colour
Pair each of 3¹⁄₄mm (UK No 10/US size 3) and 3³⁄₄mm (UK No 9/US size 5) knitting needles
Cable needle
6(7:8) buttons

SIZES AND MEASUREMENTS

To fit ages	1	2	3	years
Finished knitted measurements				
Length to shoulder	39	43	48	cm
	15¹⁄₂	17	19	in
Sleeve length	24	26	28	cm
	9¹⁄₂	10¹⁄₄	11	in

TENSION

23 sts and 31 rows to 10cm/4in over st st using 3³⁄₄mm (UK No 9/US size 5) needles.

ABBREVIATIONS

C2B (cable 2 back) = slip next st onto a cable needle and leave at back of work, k1, then k1 from cable needle
C2F (cable 2 front) = slip next st onto a cable needle and leave at front of work, k1, then k1 from cable needle
Cr2L (cross 2 left) = slip next st onto a cable needle and leave at front of work, p1, then k1 from cable needle
Cr2R (cross 2 right) = slip next st onto a cable needle and leave at back of work, k1, then p1 from cable needle.
See also page 21.

BACK

With 3¹⁄₄mm (No 10/US 3) needles and main colour, cast on 105(115:125) sts.
1st moss st row (RS) K1, *p1, k1; rep from * to end.
Rep last row 5 times more, so ending with a WS row.
Change to 3³⁄₄mm (No 9/US 5) needles, and beg with a k row, work in st st until back measures 28(31:35)cm/11(12¹⁄₄:13³⁄₄)in from cast-on edge, ending with a RS row.
Next row (dec row) (WS) P2(3:3), [p2tog, p2, p2tog, p3] 11(12:13) times, p2tog, p2(2:3). 82(90:98) sts.
Yoke
1st row (RS) P4, [C2F, p6] to last 6 sts, C2F, p4.
2nd row K3, [Cr2L, Cr2R, k4] to last 7 sts, Cr2L, Cr2R, k3.
3rd row P2, [Cr2R, p2, Cr2L, p2] to end.
4th row K1, [Cr2L, k4, Cr2R] to last st, k1.

5th row P1, k1, [p6, C2B] to last 8 sts, p6, k1, p1.
6th row K1, [Cr2R, k4, Cr2L] to last st, k1.
7th row P2, [Cr2L, p2, Cr2R, p2] to end.
8th row K3, [Cr2R, Cr2L, k4] to last 7 sts, Cr2R, Cr2L, k3.
The last 8 rows form the yoke patt.
Work in yoke patt until back measures 39(43:48)cm/15¹⁄₂(17:19)in from beg, ending with a RS row.
Shape Neck and Shoulder
Keeping patt correct as set throughout and casting off in patt, divide for neck on next row as foll:
Next row (WS) Work 30(33:36) sts in patt, cast off next 22(24:26) sts for centre back neck, work in patt to end.
Working on this set of sts only for first side of neck, cast off 8(9:10) sts at beg of next row and 3 sts at beg of foll row, so ending with a WS row.
Rep last 2 rows once more.
Cast off rem 8(9:10) sts.
With RS facing, rejoin yarn to rem sts, then work in patt to end.
Complete to match first side.

LEFT FRONT

With 3¹⁄₄mm (No 10/US 3) needles and main colour, cast on 59(65:71) sts.
1st moss st row (RS) K1, *p1, k1; rep from * to end.
Rep last row 5 times more, so ending with a WS row.
Change to 3³⁄₄mm (No 9/US 5) needles and beg st st with moss st button band as foll:
Next row (RS) K to last 4 sts, work 4 sts in moss st.
Next row Work 4 sts in moss st, p to end.
Rep last 2 rows until front matches back to dec row before beg of yoke patt, ending with a RS row.
Next row (dec row) (WS) Work 4 sts in moss st, [p2tog, p2] to last 3(9:15) sts, [p2tog, p1] 1(3:5) times. 45(49:53) sts.
Yoke
1st row (RS) P4, [C2F, p6] to last 9(13:9) sts, C2F, p3(6:3), k0(1:0), work 4 sts in moss st.
2nd row Work 4 sts in moss st, [Cr2R] 0(1:0) time, k2(4:2), [Cr2L, Cr2R, k4] to last 7 sts, Cr2L, Cr2R, k3.
3rd row P2, [Cr2R, p2, Cr2L, p2] to last 11(7:11) sts, [Cr2R, p2, Cr2L, p1] 1(0:1) time, [Cr2R, p1] 0(1:0) time, work 4 sts in moss st.
4th row Work 4 sts in moss st, [k2, Cr2R] 0(1:0) time, [Cr2L, k4, Cr2R] to last st, k1.
5th row P1, k1, [p6, C2B] to last 11(7:11) sts, p6(3:6), k1(0:1), work 4 sts in moss st.
6th row Work 4 sts in moss st, [k2, Cr2L] 0(1:0) time, [Cr2R, k4, Cr2L] to last st, k1.
7th row P2, [Cr2L, p2, Cr2R, p2] to last 11(7:11) sts, Cr2L, p2(1:2), [Cr2R, p1] 1(0:1) time, work 4 sts in moss st.
8th row Work 4 sts in moss st, [Cr2L] 0(1:0) time, k2(4:2), [Cr2R, Cr2L, k4] to last 7 sts, Cr2R, Cr2L, k3.
The last 8 rows form the yoke patt with the moss st band.
Work in patt until front measures 36(39:43)cm/14¹⁄₄(15¹⁄₄:17)in from beg, ending with a RS row.

Shape Neck

Keeping patt correct as set throughout and casting off in patt, cast off 11(12:13) sts at beg of next row and 4 sts at beg of 2 foll alt rows, so ending with a WS row. 26(29:32) sts.

Dec one st at neck edge on next 2 rows. 24(27:30) sts.

Work without shaping until front matches back to shoulder shaping, ending at armhole edge.

Shape Shoulder

Cast off 8(9:10) sts at beg of next row and foll alt row.

Work one row without shaping.

Cast off rem 8(9:10) sts.

Mark positions of buttons on button band, the first one 16cm/6¼in above cast-on edge, the last 5mm/¼in from neck edge and the rem 4(5:6) evenly spaced between.

RIGHT FRONT

With 3¼mm (No 10/US 3) needles and main colour, cast on 59(65:71) sts.

1st moss st row (RS) K1, *p1, k1; rep from * to end.

Rep last row 5 times more, so ending with a WS row.

Change to 3¾mm (No 9/US 5) needles and beg st st with moss st buttonhole band as foll:

Next row (RS) Work 4 sts in moss st, k to end.

Next row P to last 4 sts, work 4 sts in moss st.

Rep last 2 rows until front measures 16cm/6¼in from cast-on edge, ending with a WS row.

Keeping to st st patt and moss st buttonhole band as set, work first buttonhole as foll:

Next row (buttonhole row) (RS) Work 2 sts in moss st, yf, work 2 sts tog, work in patt to end.

Cont in st st with moss st buttonhole band, working buttonholes when reached, until front matches back to dec row before beg of yoke patt, ending with a RS row.

Next row (dec row) (WS) [P1, p2tog] 1(3:5) times, [p2, p2tog], to last 4 sts, work 4 sts in moss st. 45(49:53) sts.

Yoke

1st row (RS) Work 4 sts in moss st, k0(1:0), p3(6:3), C2F, [p6, C2F] to last 4 sts, p4.

2nd row K3, Cr2L, Cr2R, [k4, Cr2L, Cr2R] to last 6(10:6) sts, k2(4:2), [Cr2L] 0(1:0) time, work 4 sts in moss st.

These 2 rows set position of yoke patt.

Complete to match left front, working buttonholes when reached.

SLEEVES (make 2)

With 3¼mm (No 10/US 3) needles and main colour, cast on 34(42:50) sts.

For cuff, work 9 rows in yoke patt as given for back.

Change to 3¾mm (No 9/US 5) needles and st st.

Next row (WS) P3, m1, *p4, m1, [p2, m1] twice; rep from * to last 7 sts, p4, m1, [p2, m1] 1(0:1) time, p1(3:1). 46(56:68) sts.

Cont in st st, inc one st at each end of every foll 4th row until there are 68(82:96) sts, so ending with a RS row.

Work 5(3:5) rows in st st without shaping, so ending with a WS row.

Beg yoke patt panel on next row as foll:

Next row (RS) K17(20:23), work 1st row of yoke patt as given for back across next 34(42:50) sts, k17(20:23).

Next row P17(20:23), work 2nd row of yoke patt as given for back across next 34(42:50) sts, p17(20:23).

Work 15 rows more in patt as set.

Cast off.

COLLAR

With 3¼mm (No 10/US 3) needles and main colour, cast on 59(67:75) sts.

1st moss st row (RS) K1, *p1, k1; rep from * to end.

Rep last row 5 times more, so ending with WS row.

Change to 3¾mm (No 9/US 5) needles and beg patt as foll:

1st row (RS) Work 2 sts in moss st, p4, C2F, p4, k35(43:51), p4, C2F, p4, work 2 sts in moss st.

2nd row Work 2 sts in moss st, k3, Cr2L, Cr2R, k3, p35(43:51), k3, Cr2L, Cr2R, k3, work 2 sts in moss st.

3rd row Work 2 sts in moss st, p2, Cr2R, p2, Cr2L, p2, k35(43:51), p2, Cr2R, p2, Cr2L, p2, work 2 sts in moss st.

4th row Work 2 sts in moss st, k1, Cr2L, k4, Cr2R, k1, p35(43:51), k1, Cr2L, k4, Cr2R, k1, work 2 sts in moss st.

5th row Work 2 sts in moss st, p1, k1, p6, k1, p1, k35(43:51), p1, k1, p6, k1, p1, work 2 sts in moss st.

6th row Work 2 sts in moss st, k1, Cr2R, k4, Cr2L, k1, p35(43:51), k1, Cr2R, k4, Cr2L, k1, work 2 sts in moss st.

7th row Work 2 sts in moss st, p2, Cr2L, p2, Cr2R, p2, k35(43:51), p2, Cr2L, p2, Cr2R, p2, work 2 sts in moss st.

8th row Work 2 sts in moss st, k3, Cr2R, Cr2L, k3, p35(43:51), k3, Cr2R, Cr2L, k3, work 2 sts in moss st.

The last 8 rows form the collar patt.

Work 19(23:27) rows more in patt as set, so ending with a RS row.

Shape Neck

Keeping patt correct as set throughout and casting off in patt, divide for neck on next row as foll:

Next row (WS) Work 20(23:26) sts in patt, cast off next 19(21:23) sts, work in patt to end.

Working on this set of sts only for right side of collar, dec one st at neck edge on next 4 rows.

Work 8 rows without shaping.

Inc one st at neck edge on next 6 rows.

Work one row without shaping, so ending at neck edge.

Next row Cast on 7(8:9) sts, k1, p1, work in patt to end. 29(33:37) sts.

Next row Work in patt to last 2 sts, p1, k1.

Work 16(20:24) rows more.

Work 6 rows in moss st (across all sts).

Cast off in moss st.

With RS facing, rejoin yarn to rem sts, then complete left collar to match right collar.

TO MAKE UP

Join shoulder seams. Sew on sleeves, matching centre of sleeve to shoulder seam. Join side and sleeve seams. Sew on collar. Sew on buttons.

Embroidery

Using contrast colour, embroider smocking effect on smock patt areas of bodice, collar and top of sleeves by working 2 back sts over each C2B and C2F and where appropriate at side edges level with these cables.

Rather than breaking off the yarn after each embroidered sttich, run the yarn along the crossed stitches at the back, making sure it doesn't show through.

Embroidered Denim Jacket

A shaped jacket in fading denim yarn is an ideal base for folkloric-style embroidery. It has a back vent, and the sleeves have folded back, shirt-style cuffs.

MATERIALS

15(16:17) x 50g (1¾oz) balls of Rowan *Denim*

Pair each of 3¾mm (UK No 9/US size 5) and 4mm (UK No 8/ US size 6) knitting needles

Yarn for embroidery – small amount each of double-knitting-weight or tapestry-weight wool yarn in Red, Rust, Light Blue, White, Light Green and Dark Green

8 buttons

SIZES AND MEASUREMENTS

To fit bust	82	86	92	cm
	32	34	36	in
Finished knitted measurements (after washing)				
Around bust	101	105	109	cm
	39¾	41¼	43	in
Length to shoulder	54	56	58	cm
	21¼	22	23	in
Sleeve length (with cuff turned back)				
	42	43	44	cm
	16½	17	17½	in

TENSION BEFORE WASHING

See basic information about denim yarn on page 11.

20 sts and 28 rows to 10cm/4in over st st using 4mm (UK No 8/ US size 6) needles.

ABBREVIATIONS

dec2tog (decrease 2 together) = slip next 2 sts off needle together knitwise (as if to k them together), k next st, then pass 2 slipped sts over the knit st and off the needle.

See also page 21.

BACK

The back has a short vent at the centre back, so it is worked in two sections to the top of the vent, then the sections are joined.

Right Back Section

With 3¾mm (No 9/US 5) needles, cast on 53(55:57) sts.

1st moss st row (WS) K1, *p1, k1; rep from * to end.

Rep last row 6 times more.

Change to 4mm (No 8/US 6) needles and work right back in st st with moss st edging for vent as foll:

Next row (RS) K to last 4 sts, [p1, k1] twice.

Next row [K1, p1] twice, k1, p to end.

Rep last 2 rows 15 times more, so ending with a WS row.

Next row (RS) K to last 5 sts, cast off these 5 sts. Break off yarn and fasten off.

Leave rem 48(50:52) sts on a spare needle.

Left Back Section

With 3¾mm (No 9/US 5) needles, cast on 53(55:57) sts.

1st moss st row (WS) K1, *p1, k1; rep from * to end.

Rep last row 6 times more.

Change to 4mm (No 8/US 6) needles and work left back in st st with moss st edging for vent as foll:

Next row (RS) [K1, p1] twice, k to end.

Next row P to last 5 sts, k1, [p1, k1] twice.

Rep last 2 rows 15 times more, so ending with a WS row.

Next row (RS) [K1, p1] twice, k to end.

Join Left and Right Back Sections

Join left back to right back on next row as foll:

Next row (WS) P across sts of left back, then with WS of right back facing, p across sts of right back. 101(105:109) sts.

Shape Back

Working in st st throughout, beg shaping back as foll:

Next row (RS) K24(25:26), dec2tog, k47(49:51), dec2tog, k24(25:26). 97(101:105) sts.

Work 3 rows without shaping.

Next row K23(24:25), dec2tog, k45(47:49), dec2tog, k23(24:25). 93(97:101) sts.

Work 3 rows without shaping.

Next row K22(23:24), dec2tog, k43(45:47), dec2tog, k22(23:24). 89(93:97) sts.

Work 3 rows without shaping.

Next row K21(22:23), dec2tog, k41(43:45), dec2tog, k21(22:23). 85(89:93) sts.

Work 3 rows without shaping.

Next row K20(21:22), dec2tog, k39(41:43), dec2tog, k20(21:22). 81(85:89) sts.

Work 3 rows without shaping.

Next row K19(20:21), dec2tog, k37(39:41), dec2tog, k19(20:21). 77(81:85) sts.

Work 3 rows without shaping.

Next row K18(19:20), dec2tog, k35(37:39), dec2tog, k18(19:20). 73(77:81) sts.

Work 3 rows without shaping.

Next row K17(18:19), dec2tog, k33(35:37), dec2tog, k17(18:19). 69(73:77) sts.

Work 3(5:7) rows without shaping.

Next row K17(18:19), m1, k1, m1, k33(35:37), m1, k1, m1, k17(18:19). 73(77:81) sts.

Work 3 rows without shaping.

Next row K18(19:20), m1, k1, m1, k35(37:39), m1, k1, m1, k18(19:20). 77(81:85) sts.

Work 3 rows without shaping.

Next row K19(20:21), m1, k1, m1, k37(39:41), m1, k1, m1, k19(20:21). 81(85:89) sts.

Work 3 rows without shaping.

Next row K20(21:22), m1, k1, m1, k39(41:43), m1, k1, m1, k20(21:22). 85(89:93) sts.

Work 3 rows without shaping.

Next row K21(22:23), m1, k1, m1, k41(43:45), m1, k1, m1, k21(22:23). 89(93:97) sts.

Work 3 rows without shaping.

Next row K22(23:24), m1, k1, m1, k43(45:47), m1, k1, m1, k22(23:24). 93(97:101) sts.

Work 3 rows without shaping.

Next row K23(24:25), m1, k1, m1, k45(47:49), m1, k1, m1, k23(24:25). 97(101:105) sts.

Work 3 rows without shaping.

Next row K24(25:26), m1, k1, m1, k47(49:51), m1, k1, m1, k24(25:26). 101(105:109) sts.

Work without shaping until back measures 42(43:44)cm/16½ (17:17¼)in from cast-on edge, ending with a WS row.

Shape Armholes

Cast off 7(8:9) sts at beg of next 2 rows and 2 sts on the foll 4 rows.

Dec one st at each end of next row and 2 foll alt rows. 73(75:77) sts.

Work without shaping until back measures 67(69:71)cm/26½ (27¼:28)in from cast-on edge, ending with a WS row.

Shape Shoulders

Cast off 11 sts at beg of next 4 rows.

Cast off rem 29(31:33) sts.

LEFT FRONT

With 3¾mm (No 9/US 5) needles, cast on 53(55:57) sts.

1st moss st row (WS) K1, *p1, k1; rep from * to end.

Rep last row 6 times more.

Change to 4mm (No 8/US 6) needles and work front in st st with moss st edging for button band as foll:

Next row (RS) K to last 4 sts, [p1, k1] twice.

Next row [K1, p1] twice, k1, p to end.

These last 2 rows set the st st patt with a 5-st moss st button band.

Work 32 rows more in patt as set, so ending with a WS row.

Shape Left Front

Cont in patt as set throughout, shape left front as foll:

Next row (RS) K24(25:26), dec2tog, k22(23:24), [p1, k1] twice. 51(53:55) sts.

Work 3 rows without shaping.

Next row K23(24:25), dec2tog, k21(22:23), [p1, k1] twice. 49(51:53) sts.

Work 3 rows without shaping.

Next row K22(23:24), dec2tog, k20(21:22), [p1, k1] twice. 47(49:51) sts.

Don't worry too much if your embroidery technique isn't perfect – your stitches will have a charm and originality of their own.

Work 3 rows without shaping.

Next row K21(22:23), dec2tog, k19(20:21), [p1, k1] twice. 45(47:49) sts.

Work 3 rows without shaping.

Next row K20(21:22), dec2tog, k18(19:20), [p1, k1] twice. 43(45:47) sts.

Work 3 rows without shaping.

Next row K19(20:21), dec2tog, k17(18:19), [p1, k1] twice. 41(43:45) sts.

Work 3 rows without shaping.

Next row K18(19:20), dec2tog, k16(17:18), [p1, k1] twice. 39(41:43) sts.

Work 3 rows without shaping.

Next row K17(18:19), dec2tog, k15(16:17), [p1, k1] twice. 37(39:41) sts.

Work 3(5:7) rows without shaping.

Next row K17(18:19), m1, k1, m1, k15(16:17), [p1, k1] twice. 39(41:43) sts.

Work 3 rows without shaping.

Next row K18(19:20), m1, k1, m1, k16(17:18), [p1, k1] twice. 41(43:45) sts.

Work 3 rows without shaping.

Next row K19(20:21), m1, k1, m1, k17(18:19), [p1, k1] twice. 43(45:47) sts.

Work 3 rows without shaping.

Next row K20(21:22), m1, k1, m1, k18(19:20), [p1, k1] twice. 45(47:49) sts.

Work 3 rows without shaping.

Next row K21(22:23), m1, k1, m1, k19(20:21), [p1, k1] twice. 47(49:51) sts.

Work 3 rows without shaping.

Next row K22(23:24), m1, k1, m1, k20(21:22), [p1, k1] twice. 49(51:53) sts.

Work 3 rows without shaping.

Next row K23(24:25), m1, k1, m1, k21(22:23), [p1, k1] twice. 51(53:55) sts.

Work 3 rows without shaping.

Next row K24(25:26), m1, k1, m1, k22(23:24), [p1, k1] twice. 53(55:57) sts.

Work without shaping until front matches back to armhole shaping, ending with a WS row at armhole edge.

Shape Armhole

Cast off 7(8:9) sts at beg of next row.

Cast off 2 sts at beg (armhole edge) of 2 foll alt rows.

Dec one st at beg (armhole edge) of 3 foll alt rows. 39(40:41) sts.

Work without shaping until front measures 58(59:60)cm/22¾ (23:23½)in from cast-on edge, ending with a RS row.

Shape Neck

Cast off 4 sts at beg of next row and foll alt row.

Dec one st at neck edge on next 5 rows, and then on every foll alt row until 22 sts rem.

Work without shaping until front matches back to shoulder shaping, ending with a WS row at armhole edge.

Shape Shoulder

Cast off 11 sts at beg of next row.

Work one row without shaping. Cast off rem 11 sts.

Mark positions of buttons on button band, the first one 2cm/³⁄₄in above cast-on edge, the last 1cm/¹⁄₂in from neck edge, and the rem 6 evenly spaced between.

RIGHT FRONT

With 3³⁄₄mm (No 9/US 5) needles, cast on 53(55:57) sts.

1st moss st row K1, *p1, k1; rep from * to end.

Work each buttonhole on a RS row when reached as foll:

Buttonhole row (RS) K1, p1, k2tog, yf, k1, work in patt to end.

And at the same time, cont working right front as foll:

Rep first moss st row 6 times more.

Change to 4mm (No 8/US 6) needles and work front in st st with moss st buttonhole band as foll:

Next row (RS) [K1, p1] twice, k to end.

Next row P to last 5 sts, k1, [p1, k1] twice.

These last 2 rows set the st st patt with a 5-st moss st buttonhole band.

Work 32 rows more in patt as set, so ending with a WS row.

Shape Right Front

Cont in patt as set throughout, beg shaping right front as foll:

Next row (RS) [K1, p1] twice, k22(23:24), dec2tog, k24(25:26). 51(53:55) sts.

Work 3 rows without shaping.

Next row [K1, p1] twice, k21(22:23), dec2tog, k23(24:25). 49(51:53) sts.

Work 3 rows without shaping.

Complete to match left front, reversing all shaping and cont to work buttonholes when reached.

SLEEVES (make 2)

The cuff has a short slit at the centre, so it is worked in two sections to the top of the slit, then the two sections are joined.

First half of cuff

With 3³⁄₄mm (No 9/US 5) needles, cast on 24(26:28) sts.

1st moss st row K1, *p1, k1; rep from * to end.

Rep last row 5 times more.

Next row (dec row) Work in moss st to last 2 sts, work 2 sts tog.

Keeping moss stitch correct as set, work 5 rows without shaping.

Next row (dec row) Work in moss st to last 2 sts, work 2 sts tog.

Rep last 6 rows once more. 21(23:25) sts.

Work one row in moss st without shaping.

Leave these sts on a spare needle.

Second Half of Cuff

With 3³⁄₄mm (No 9/US 5) needles, cast on 24(26:28) sts.

1st moss st row K1, *p1, k1; rep from * to end.

Rep last row 5 times more.

Next row (dec row) Work 2 sts tog, work in moss st to end.

Keeping moss stitch correct as set, work 5 rows without shaping.

Next row (dec row) Work 2 sts tog, work in moss st to end.

Rep last 6 rows once more. 21(23:25) sts.

Work one row in moss st without shaping.

Join Two Sections of Cuff

Next row Work 20(22:24) sts in moss st, work last st of second half of cuff tog with first st of first half, then work 20(22:24) sts in moss st. 41(45:49) sts.

Work 33 rows more in moss st.

Change to 4mm (No 8/US 6) needles.

Working in st st throughout, inc one st at each end of next row and then every foll 7th row until there are 71(77:83) sts.

Work without shaping until sleeve measures 61(63:65)cm/24 (24³⁄₄:25¹⁄₂)in from cast-on edge, ending with a WS row.

Shape Sleeve Top

Cast off 7(8:9) sts at beg of next 2 rows.

Cast off 2 sts at beg of next 2 rows.

Dec one st each end of next row and then every foll 4th row until 33(37:41) sts rem.

Dec one st at each end of 1(3:3) foll alt rows.

Dec one st at each end of next 5(5:7) rows.

Cast off 3 sts at beg of next 2 rows.

Cast off rem 15 sts.

COLLAR

With 3³⁄₄mm (No 9/US 5) needles, cast on 83(87:91) sts.

1st row (RS) K3, p1, *k1, p1; rep from * to last 3 sts, k3.

2nd row K1, p2, k2, *p1, k1; rep from * to last 4 sts, k1, p2, k1.

3rd row (inc row) K3, p1, m1, work in moss st to last 4 sts, m1, p1, k3.

4th row K1, p2, k1, work in moss st to last 4 sts, k1, p2, k1.

5th row K3, p1, work in moss st to last 4 sts, p1, k3.

6th row (inc row) K1, p2, k1, m1, work in moss st to last 4 sts, m1, k1, p2, k1.

7th row As row 5.

8th row As row 4.

Rep 3rd–8th rows 3 times more, then 3rd and 4th rows again.

Cast off in patt.

TO MAKE UP

Join shoulder seams.

Wash pieces according to yarn label and instructions for denim yarn on page 11.

Sew in sleeves. Join side and sleeve seams. Sew on buttons.

Sew cast-off sts on centre back vent to WS.

Sew cast-on edge of collar to neck edge, placing edges of collar halfway across front bands.

Embroidery

Using satin stitch, stem stitch and French knots, work embroidery on cuffs and collar as shown in diagram below. (See pages 86 and 87 for how to work stitches.)

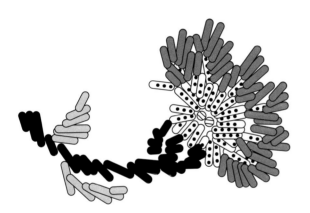 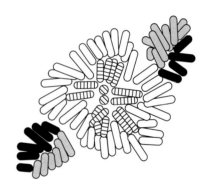

Key

Red satin stitch

Rust satin stitch

Light Blue satin stitch

White satin stitch

Dark Green stem stitch

Light Green satin stitch

Red French Knots

Embroidered Bag

Designed by Pam Allen, this simple cotton bag is decorated with the most exquisite embroidery. For a more dramatic look, you could use a black background.

MATERIALS

1 x 50g (1³⁄₄oz) ball of Jaeger *Pure Cotton*
Stranded cotton embroidery floss in Pale Salmon, Light Salmon, Mid Salmon, Light Pink, Dark Pink, Red, Light Coral, Dark Green and Light Green
Pair of 3mm (UK No 11/US size 3) knitting needles
Two 3mm (UK No 11/US size 3) double-pointed knitting needles
18 x 18cm/7¹⁄₄ x 7¹⁄₄in piece of lightweight iron-on interfacing

MEASUREMENTS

Approximate size 18 x 17cm/7¹⁄₄ x 6¹⁄₂in

TENSION

27 sts and 34 rows to 10cm/4in over st st using 3mm (UK No 11/US size 3) needles.

ABBREVIATIONS

See page 21.

TO MAKE

With 3mm (No 11/US 3) needles, cast on 49 sts.
1st moss st row K1, *p1, k1; rep from * to end.
Rep last row twice more.
Beg with a k row, work 54 rows in st st, so ending with a WS (purl) row.
Next row (RS) P to end to form foldline ridge.
Beg with a p row, work 54 rows in st st.
Work 3 rows in moss st.
Cast off in patt.

CORD

With 3mm (No 11/US 3) double-pointed needles, cast on 4 sts.
1st row (RS) K to end. (Do not turn.)
2nd row (RS) With RS still facing, slide sts back to beg of double-pointed needle, then take yarn across back of work to beg of row and k first st tightly, k to end. (Do not turn.)
Rep 2nd row until cord measures 36cm/14in from cast-on edge.
Cast off. (See page 116 for more information about this cord.)

The bag is knitted on a smaller needle than usual for this yarn, to prevent it becoming shapeless and for a good firm base for the embroidery.

EMBROIDERY

Copy motif onto lightweight iron-on interfacing and position on one side of bag. Gently touch warm iron to interfacing to make it stick only temporarily.

Stitching over motif outlines through interfacing and knitting, work embroidery as foll:

First, work centre petals of large flower in satin stitch, using four strands of Pale Salmon for one section, four strands of Light Salmon for another section and Light Pink for a third section. Work outer petals by shading with Light Salmon, Dark Pink and Red.

Using two strands of Dark Green, work stems in stem stitch.

Using three strands of Light Green or Dark Green, work leaves in satin stitch.

Use four strands of embroidery thread to work French knot flower buds, using Pale Salmon, Light Salmon, Light Coral, Dark Pink and Red as desired.

Work French knots at centre of large flower with a single knot at centre in Light Green and surrounding knots in Light Coral and Mid Salmon.

When embroidery is complete, cut away excess interfacing, using sharp scissors. (See pages 86 and 87 for how to work stitches.)

TO MAKE UP

Join side seams. Sew ends of cord to inside of seams.

Edgings on Knitting
Lacy, scalloped or simple, decorative edgings offer a pretty alternative to traditional knitted borders

Edgings basics

The interesting shapes of knitted edgings are formed using the basic techniques of increasing and decreasing. Yarn overs create the lacy eyelets (see page 18 for how to make eyelets). This selection of edging patterns includes some worked vertically and some worked horizontally. Eyelet Daisy Edging, Narrow Lace Edging, Bobble and Lace Edging and Faggoting with Zigzag are knit as strips that are sewn onto the finished knitting, while Scalloped Bobble Edge and Chevron Lace can be worked directly onto your knitting. Small Picot Edge is a simple decorative cast off. All are easy to work and make good exercises for practising edgings.

EYELET DAISY EDGING

Cast on 12 sts.

1st row (RS) K1, yf, k2tog, k6, yf, k2tog, k1.
2nd row K12.
3rd row K1, yf, k2, k2tog, yrn twice, k2tog, k2, yf, k2tog, k1.
4th row K7, yf, k2tog, k4.
5th row K1, yf, k1, k2tog, yrn twice, k2tog twice, yrn twice, k2tog, yf, k2tog, k1.
6th row K5, yf, k2tog, k2, yf, k2tog, k3.
7th row K1, yf, k4, k2tog, yrn twice, k2tog, k2, yf, k2tog, k1.
8th row K7, yf, k2tog, k6.
9th row K1, yf, k3tog, k2tog, yrn twice, k2tog twice, yrn twice, k2tog, yf, k2tog, k1.
10th row As 6th row.
11th row K1, yf, k3tog, k1, k2tog, yrn twice, k2tog, k2, yf, k2tog, k1.
12th row As 4th row.
13th row K1, yf, k3tog, k6, yf, k2tog, k1.
14th row K12.
These 14 rows form the patt and are repeated throughout.

NARROW LACE EDGING

Cast on 6 sts.

1st row (RS) K1, k2tog, yf, k2, yrn twice to make a double yarn over, k1.
2nd row K1, k1 and k1 tbl both into double yarn over, k2tog, yf, k3.
3rd row K1, k2tog, yf, k5.
4th row Cast off 2 sts, then k2tog, yf, k3.
These 4 rows form the patt and are repeated throughout.

BOBBLE AND LACE EDGING

Cast on 12 sts.

1st row (WS) K4, yf, sl 1, k2tog, psso, yf, k3, yf, k2.
2nd row K4, [k1, p1] 3 times all in next st, p2, k6.
3rd row K4, yf, skpo, k2tog, cast off 5 sts, k2, yf, k2.
4th row K5, yf, k1, p1, k6.
5th row K4, yf, sl 1, k2tog, psso, yf, k3, yf, k2tog, yf, k2.
6th row K6, [k1, p1] 3 times all in next st, p2, k6.
7th row K4, yf, skpo, k2tog, cast off 5 sts, k2, yf, k2tog, yf, k2.
8th row Cast off 4 sts, k2, yf, k1, p1, k6.
These 8 rows form the patt and are repeated throughout

SCALLOPED BOBBLE EDGE

Worked over a multiple of 10 sts, plus 1 extra.

1st row (WS) K to end.
2nd row K5, [k1, p1, k1, p1, k1] all in next st, [turn, k5, turn, p5] twice, then pass 2nd, 3rd, 4th and 5th sts over first st— called *make bobble* or *mb*—, *k9, mb; rep from * to last 5 sts, k5.
3rd and 4th rows K to end.
5th row P1, *yrn, p3, p3tog tbl, p3, yrn, p1; rep from * to end.
6th row K2, *yf, k2, sl 1, k2tog, psso, k2, yf, k3; rep from * to last 9 sts, yf, k2, sl 1, k2tog, psso, k2, yf, k2.
7th row P3, *yrn, p1, p3tog tbl, p1, yrn, p5; rep from * to last 8 sts, yrn, p1, p3tog tbl, p1, yrn, p3.
8th row K4, *yf, sl 1, k2tog, psso, yf, k7; rep from * to last 7 sts, yf, sl 1, k2tog, psso, k4.
9th row P to end.
10th–13th rows K to end.
Cast off, or if desired, beg main piece of knitting.

TRIANGLE BOBBLE EDGING
Worked over a multiple of 9 sts.
1st row (WS) K to end.
2nd and 3rd rows K to end.
**4th row (RS) K9, turn (and cont to work on these sts only for 5th–11th rows).
5th row K2tog tbl, k5, k2tog.
6th row K3, [K1, p1, k1, p1, k1, p1, k1] all in next st, then pass 2nd, 3rd, 4th, 5th, 6th and 7th sts over first st, k3.
7th row K2tog tbl, k3, k2tog.
8th row K5.
9th row K2tog tbl, k1, k2tog.
10th row K3.
11th row Sl 1, k2tog, psso.
Fasten off.
With RS facing, rejoin yarn to rem sts.**
Rep from ** to ** until all sts have been worked.
Cast off, or if desired, beg main piece of knitting.
Alternative versions: Work in moss stitch or leave off the bobbles.
This edging is worked from a cast-on edge. It can be picked up and knitted down from the hem, but lies flatter if sewn on afterwards.

SMALL PICOT EDGE
Worked over an odd number of sts on the cast-off row.
Cast off row (RS) Cast off one st knitwise, *slip st used in casting off back onto left-hand needle, cast on 2 sts knitwise, cast off 4 sts knitwise; rep from * to end.
Fasten off.
Alternative version: To make the edging more delicate, try casting off 6 sts (see Floral Cardigan on page 81).

FAGGOTING WITH ZIGZAG
Cast on 8 sts. K one row.
1st row Sl 1, k1, [yf, k2tog] twice, yf, k2.
2nd row K2, yf, k2, [yf, k2tog] twice, k1.
3rd row Sl 1, k1, [yf, k2tog] twice, k2, yf, k2.
4th row K2, yf, k4, [yf, k2tog] twice, k1.
5th row Sl 1, k1, [yf, k2tog] twice, k4, yf, k2.
6th row K2, yf, k6, [yf, k2tog] twice, k1.
7th row Sl 1, k1, [yf, k2tog] twice, k6, yf, k2.
8th row K2, yf, k8, [yf, k2tog] twice, k1.
9th row Sl 1, k1, [yf, k2tog] twice, k8, yf, k2.
10th row K2, yf, k10, [yf, k2tog] twice, k1.
11th row Sl 1, k1, [yf, k2tog] twice, k10, yf, k2.
12th row Cast off 11 sts, k2, [yf, k2tog] twice, k1.
These 12 rows form the patt and are repeated throughout.

CHEVRON LACE
Worked over a multiple 16 sts, plus 17 extra.
1st row (RS) Skpo, *p2, k2, p2, yon, k1, yrn, p2, k2, p2, yb, insert right-hand needle knitwise into 2nd st then first st on left-hand needle and slip these 2 sts, k1, then pass 2 slipped sts over—called *slip 2, knit one, pass slipped stitches over* or *s2kpsso*—; rep from * to last 15 sts, p2, k2, p2, yon, k1, yrn, p2, k2, p2, k2tog.
2nd row P1, *k2, p2, k2, p3, k2, p2, k2, p1; rep from * to end.
3rd row Skpo, *p1, k2, p2, k1, [yf, k1] twice, p2, k2, p1, yb, s2kpsso; rep from * to last 15 sts, p1, k2, p2, k1, [yf, k1] twice, p2, k2, p1, k2tog.
4th row P1, *k1, p2, k2, p5, k2, p2, k1, p1; rep from * to end.
5th row Skpo, *k2, p2, k2, yf, k1, yf, k2, p2, k2, s2kpsso; rep from * to last 15 sts, k2, p2, k2, yf, k1, yf, k2, p2, k2, k2tog.
6th row P3, *k2, p7, k2, p5; rep from * to last 14 sts, k2, p7, k2, p3.
7th row Skpo, *k1, p2, k2, p1, yon, k1, yrn, p1, k2, p2, k1, s2kpsso; rep from * to last 15 sts, k1, p2, k2, p1, yon, k1, yrn, p1, k2, p2, k1, k2tog.
8th row P2, *k2, p2, k1, p3, k1, p2, k2, p3; rep from * to last 15 sts, k2, p2, k1, p3, k1, p2, k2, p2.
Cast off, or if desired, beg main piece of knitting.

Edgings class

The edgings given on the previous two pages would all make beautiful additions to a knitted garment, blanket or cushion. The trick is to marry the right edging with the right main stitch texture. Here is how I approach adding edgings to my knits.

'Framing' your knitwear

When designing a garment, I get a great deal of satisfaction thinking about how I will 'frame' it. By this, I mean that the borders or edges of the design are as important to me as the patterning on the body. In some cases, I might be deciding how to run cables down into the ribbed welts (see Texture Detailing Class on page 44). But more often than not, I will be looking at the wonderful edging patterns that are available to knitters. Some of these can be worked up from the cast-on edge of the garment, but many of them are worked vertically and then sewn on afterwards, which has some advantages. A small pattern repeat over perhaps seven or 12 stitches seems easy to tackle and workable. By sewing the edging on afterwards, it can be slightly stretched, and by using a flat seam, it will lie flat against the rest of the garment.

If you see a design that you like that has conventional ribbed borders, you can try leaving them off and sewing a decorative edge on to the cast-on row after the garment has been completed.

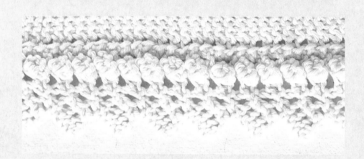

How to choose a knitted edging

I like to choose an edging that relates in some way to the rest of the design. On the garter-stitch cashmere blanket on page 109, for instance, I have used a very simple edging that is worked mainly in garter stitch as well. This particular edging can also be made to be larger or smaller, depending on how many stitches you increase to. Just make sure that you cast off back to the original amount of cast-on stitches.

You can usually customize edgings. For example, you may want to add a bobble to the one I have just mentioned, whereas the Chevron Lace pattern worked up from the cast-on row can look dramatic when worked over more repeats for a deep welt or used as a cuff or neckband. For the Floral Cardigan on page 81, I used a picot edge which is one of the very simplest you can work, as it is created only by casting on and off again on the cast-off row. Originally I wanted to convey the idea of there being a pretty lace shirt underneath the jacket, which is peeping out. However, when the garment came back I realized that the standard Picot Edge that I have used before, and here worked in white, looked crude – like sharks teeth! After initial panic, the problem was solved merely by casting off six stitches rather than the usual four, thus making a far more delicate edge. This edging can create a really pretty effect when used as the cast-off row on a ribbed collar where it produces a slightly wavy effect.

Finding inspiration for edgings

Ideas for edgings can sometimes be informed by the pattern on the main part of the knit you are designing – such as matching a particular stitch pattern like moss stitch or garter stitch – but sometimes inspiration can come from seeing an eyelet edging on a beautiful linen pillowcase, or a broderie anglaise border on a crisp cotton tablecloth.

When choosing a yarn for a baby blanket, avoid soft but hairy yarn like alpaca. The long fibres are not suitable for a small child.

Cashmere Baby Blanket

For the baby who deserves the best, here's a wrap-around cashmere baby blanket in simple garter stitch, with a distinctive triangle edging.

MATERIALS
9 x 25g (1oz) balls of Jaeger *Cashmere*
Pair of 3¼mm (UK No 10/US size 3) knitting needles

MEASUREMENTS
Approximate size (excluding edge) 54 x 67.5cm/21¼ x 26½in

ABBREVIATIONS
See page 21.

TENSION
25 sts and 46 rows to 10cm/4in over garter st using 3¼mm (UK No 10/US size 3) needles.

CENTRE SECTION
With 3¼mm (No 10/US 3) needles, cast on 135 sts.
Work in garter st until piece measures 67.5cm/26½in from cast-on edge.
Cast off.

EDGING
With 3¼mm (No 10/US 3) needles, cast on 7 sts.
1st patt row K2, yf, k2tog, yf, k to end.
2nd patt row K to end.
3rd–15th patt rows Rep 1st and 2nd rows 6 times more, then 1st row again. 15 sts.
16th patt row Cast off 8 sts, k to end.
Rep 1st–16th rows 53 times more (so there are a total of 54 peaks).

TO MAKE UP
Join cast-on and cast-off edges of edging.
Sew edging to centre section, with 12 peaks on cast-on and cast-off edges and 15 on each side.

Girl's Lace-Edged Cardigan

This slightly shaped jacket, photographed on Nell (aged 10), is a perfect style for older children who want something a little more grown up. The simple lace edging is sewn on afterwards.

MATERIALS

7(8:9:10) x 50g (1¾oz) balls of Rowan *Cotton Glacé*
Pair of 3¼mm (No UK 10/US size 3) knitting needles
7(7:8:8) buttons

SIZES AND MEASUREMENTS

To fit ages	4–5	6–7	8–9	9–10	years
Finished knitted measurements					
Around chest	69	76	81	88	cm
	27	30	32	35	in
Length to shoulder	43	45	48	50	cm
	17	17¾	19	19¾	in
Sleeve length	31	33	35	38	cm
	12¼	13	13¾	15	in

TENSION

25 sts and 40 rows to 10cm/4in over moss st using 3¼mm (UK No 10/US size 3) needles.

ABBREVIATIONS

See page 21.

BACK

With 3¼mm (No 10/US 3) needles, cast on 87(95:103:109) sts.
Beg moss st patt as foll:
1st moss st row (RS) K1, *p1, k1; rep from * to end. (Mark this first row as RS with a coloured thread.)
Rep last row to form moss st patt, work 7 rows more in moss st, so ending with a WS row.
Keeping moss st patt correct as set throughout, dec one st at each end of next row and then every foll 6th row until 75(83:89:97) sts rem.
Work without shaping until back measures 12(13:14:15)cm/4¾ (5¼:5½:6)in from cast-on edge, ending with a RS row.
Working new sts into moss st patt, inc one st at each end of next row and then every foll 6th row until there are 87(95:103:109) sts.
Work without shaping until back measures 24(26:27:29)cm/9½ (10¼:10¾:11½)in from cast-on edge, ending with a WS row.
Shape Armholes
Casting off in patt throughout, cast off 5 sts at beg of next 2 rows.
Dec one st at each end of next row and then every foll alt row until 65(71:77:83) sts rem.
Work without shaping until back measures 40(42:45:47)cm/

15¾(16½:17¾:18½)in from cast-on edge, ending with a WS row.
Shape Neck and Shoulder
Divide for neck on next row as foll:
Next row (RS) Work 22(24:26:28) sts in patt, then turn, leaving rem sts on a spare needle.
Working on this set of sts only for first side of neck, cast off 3 sts at beg of next row and 6(7:7:8) sts at beg of foll row.
Cast off 2 sts at beg of next row and 6(7:7:8) sts at beg of foll row.
Work one row without shaping.
Cast off rem 5(5:7:7) sts.
With RS facing, rejoin yarn to rem sts, cast off 21(23:25:27) sts for centre back neck, then work in patt to end.
Complete to match first side.

LEFT FRONT

With 3¼mm (No 10/ US 3) needles, cast on 43(47:51:55) sts.
Beg moss st patt as foll:
1st moss st row (RS) K1, *p1, k1; rep from * to end. (Mark this first row as RS with a coloured thread.)
Rep last row to form moss st patt, work 7 rows more in moss st, so ending with a WS row.
Keeping moss st patt correct as set throughout, dec one st at at side edge on next row and then every foll 6th row until 37(41:44: 49) sts rem.
Work without shaping until front measures 12(13:14:15)cm/4¾ (5¼:5½:6)in from cast-on edge, ending with a RS row.
Working new sts into moss st patt, inc one st at side edge on next row and then every foll 6th row until there are 43(47:51:55) sts.
Work without shaping until front matches back to armhole shaping, ending with a WS row.
Shape Armhole
Casting off in patt throughout, cast off 5 sts at beg of next row.
Work one row without shaping.
Dec one st at armhole edge on next and then every foll alt row until 32(35:38:42) sts rem.
Work without shaping until front measures 28(30:32:34)cm/11 (11¾:12½:13¼)in from cast-on edge, ending with a RS row.
Shape Neck
Dec one st at neck edge on next and then every foll alt row until 17(19:21:23) sts rem.
Work without shaping until front matches back to shoulder shaping, ending at armhole edge.
Shape Shoulder
Cast off 6(7:7:8) sts at beg of next row.
Work one row without shaping.
Rep last 2 rows once more.
Cast off rem 5(5:7:7) sts.

RIGHT FRONT

Work to match left front, reversing shaping.

SLEEVES (make 2)

With 3¼mm (No 10/ US 3) needles, cast on 41(43:47:49) sts.
Work 10 rows in moss st as given for back, so ending with a WS row.

Keeping to moss st as set throughout and working new sts into moss st patt, inc one st at each end of next row and then every foll 7th row until there are 69(73:81:85) sts.

Work without shaping until sleeve measures 28(30:32:35) cm/11 (11¾:12½:13¾)in from cast-on edge, ending with a WS row.

Shape Sleeve Top

Casting off in patt throughout, cast off 5 sts at beg of next 2 rows. 59(63:71:75) sts.

Dec one st at each end of every foll alt row until 49(51:55:57) sts rem.

Work 3 rows without shaping.

Dec one st at each end of next row and every foll 6th row until 43(45:49:51) sts rem, then every foll alt row until 39(41:45:45) sts rem.

Dec one st at each end of next 4 rows. 31(33:37:37) sts.

Cast off 4 sts at beg of next 2 rows.

Cast off rem 23(25:29:29) sts.

SLEEVE EDGINGS (make 2)

With 3¼mm (No 10/ US 3) needles, cast on 4 sts.

K one row.

1st row (RS) K2, yf, k2.

2nd row K to end.

3rd row K3, yf, k2.

4th row K to end.

5th row K2, yf, k2tog, yf, k2.

6th row K to end.

7th row K3, yf, k2tog, yf, k2.

8th row Cast off 4 sts, k to end.

The last 8 rows form edging patt.

Work in patt until edging, when slightly stretched, fits along lower edge of sleeve, ending with an 8th row.

Cast off.

TO MAKE UP

Join shoulder seams. Sew on sleeves, matching centre of sleeve to shoulder seam. Sew on sleeve edgings. Join side and sleeve seams.

LOWER EDGING

Work as given for sleeve edging until edging, when slightly stretched, fits along lower edge of back and fronts.

Sew on lower edging.

BUTTONHOLE BAND

Using 3¼mm (No 10/ US 3) needles, with RS facing and beg at lower edge on right front, pick up and k 4 sts along edging, then pick up and k 55(61:64:71) sts along front edge to neck edge. 59(65:68:75) sts.

K one row.

Work butthonholes on next row as foll:

Buttonhole row (RS) K1, [k2 tog, yf, k7(8:7:8) sts] 6(6:7:7) times, k2tog, yf, k2.

K one row.

Cast off.

BUTTON BAND

Using 3¼mm (No 10/ US 3) needles, with RS facing and beg at neck edge on right front, pick up and k 55(61:64:71) sts along front edge to cast-on edge, then pick up and k 4 sts along edging. 59(65: 68:75) sts.

K 3 rows.

Cast off.

NECK EDGING

Work as given for sleeve edging until edging, when slightly stretched, fits around neck edge.

Sew on neck edging, starting and finishing at beg of neck shaping.

Sew on buttons.

You could choose another edging to frame this simple moss stitch jacket. However, pick one that isn't too wide so that it sits neatly around the neck.

Buttons and Beads

Whether mother of pearl, crystal or wood, use buttons and beads to decorate, highlight or add glamour to your handknit designs

Beads basics

Detailing with beads can enhance a plain garment and can be used simply as an edging, or more elaborately, for example as an allover design on an evening bag. You can sew beads onto your finished piece of knitting, or knit them right in. The easiest way to knit them in is given here along with the instructions for knitting a cord for your beaded bags.

Knitting with beads

Match the weight of your yarn with the beads you are using. Beads will add weight to your garment and too heavy beads on a light yarn will make the garment sag. If you want to add beads to a chunky garment and the yarn is too thick to thread through beads, you can always sew them on afterwards. The beading method shown here uses a slipped stitch, which means that beads are placed with at least one stitch between them. On the next bead row, the beads are worked so they are staggered between those on the previous bead row – this compensates for the slipped stitches shortening the knitting on the row before.

THREADING THE BEADS ONTO THE YARN

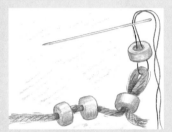

When you knit with beads, you need to thread the beads onto your yarn before you start knitting. If your yarn is thin enough, you can thread it on a needle, then pass the needle through the centre of each bead. But if your yarn is too thick to do this, use the technique for threading given here.

Fold a length of fine but strong sewing thread around the end of your knitting yarn, then thread both ends of the sewing thread through the needle. Pass the needle through the beads and push the beads over the needle and sewing thread and onto the looped yarn as shown.

KNITTING BEADS INTO STOCKING STITCH

1 On a right-side (knit) row, knit to the position for the bead. Then bring the yarn to the front of the work between the two needles and slip the next stitch purlwise.

2 Push the bead up close to the front of the knitting. Then take the yarn to the back of the work between the two needles, leaving the bead at the front. Knit the next stitch tightly to keep the bead in place.

KNITTING A CORD ON DOUBLE-POINTED NEEDLES

This is an easy way of knitting a small tubular cord. The cord can be used as decoration or for a strap on a bag. You need two double-pointed needles to make it, or a short circular needle.

Cast on 3, 4 or 5 stitches, onto a double-pointed needle. Using a second double-pointed needle, knit one row. Then without turning the work, push the stitches back to the other end of the right-hand needle. Take the yarn behind the stitches and knit the stitches again, pulling the yarn tightly when working the first stitch. Repeat the last row until the cord is the required length.

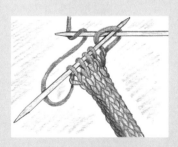

Buttons and beads class

Design possibilities for using button and bead embellishments on your knitting are endless. This is because the types of buttons and beads available are expanding all the time. If you have a collection of buttons and beads and have never been quite sure how to use them on your knitting, here are a few ideas.

Beads on knitting

Bead knitting has a great tradition historically, from intricate Victorian beaded purses to neat 1950's cardigans with beaded borders. It can add an instant touch of glamour to a simple edge on a jacket, make a perfect evening purse or be used to fringe curtains and cushions.

There are a variety of shapes and types of beads to work with: round, oval, square or faceted, in glass, metal, wood and ceramic. If your local store does not stock the variety that you need, look around in junk shops, car boot sales or flea markets – you are bound to find an unstrung necklace or two. Better still, if you are really lucky, you may find a beautiful antique beaded cardigan or a retro handbag to inspire you.

You may want to use beads on a sportier design, a chunky jacket for example. Wooden beads can look great against a heavy-weight cotton, or bright primaries against denim yarn. (On chunky knits, because of the weight of the yarn, you will probably need to sew the beads on afterwards.) Beads can also be used as details to highlight the inside of cables, or – as in the swatches below – they can be used in geometric or floral patterns. Try out your own ideas, starting with easy geometrics, by drawing out patterns on graph paper. Remember that with the beading technique on page 116, you can only bead every alternate stitch and alternate row.

The Beaded Moccasins on page 124 were inspired by my fascination with the decorative arts of Native Americans. I have been very lucky to have had many opportunities to hold workshops in America and Canada. An added bonus to this is that I have been able to visit local museums and see exquisite examples of bead and quill work. While in no way attempting to emulate the skill and craftsmanship of the pieces I saw, the moccasins are my homage to their makers.

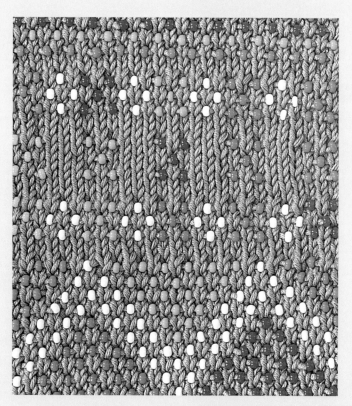

Buttons on knitting

Buttons can also be used to add decorative detailing. Cheap, tacky buttons can ruin a garment, no matter how good a quality the yarn, but the right buttons can add charm and style. There is a huge variety available now. Metallic buttons, such as pewter and bronze, can look wonderful against washed out denim. My favourite is mother of pearl. If I am unsure of the type or colour of button that would suit my design, I know I can rely on mother of pearl for quality and to pick up and reflect the shade of the yarn.

Quirky buttons can introduce some character into a knit. I particularly like the fish, tortoise and eagle buttons (below right), which I bought in the States. Children love nursery-style buttons like the goose below, and you can involve them by letting them choose their own special ones. Make sure you sew buttons on garments for babies really securely though – small children love to fiddle with them or suck them.

If a garment of yours outlives its sell-by date, before you throw it out, remember to check the buttons – you can use them again.

Beaded Cardigan

This elegant 1950's style shaped cardigan has three-quarter length sleeves. The beaded border is worked using the knitted-in beading technique.

MATERIALS

6(7:7) x 50g (1³⁄₄oz) balls of Rowan *True 4-ply Botany*
Pair each of 2³⁄₄mm (UK No 12/US size 2) and 3¹⁄₄mm
   (UK No 10/US size 3) knitting needles
Approximately 1200(1250:1300) small knitting beads
7 buttons

SIZES AND MEASUREMENTS

To fit bust	82	87	92	cm
	32	34	36	in

Finished knitted measurements

Around bust	92	97	102	cm
	36	38	40	in
Length to shoulder	51	53	55	cm
	20	21	21¹⁄₂	in
Sleeve length	29	30	31	cm
	11¹⁄₂	11³⁄₄	12¹⁄₄	in

TENSION

28 sts and 36 rows to 10cm/4in over st st on 3¹⁄₄mm (UK No 10/US size 3) needles.

ABBREVIATIONS

B1 (bead 1) = yarn to front of work, push bead up close to front of knitting, slip next st purlwise onto right-hand needle, then yarn to back of work leaving bead in front of slipped stitch.
See also page 21.

BACK

Thread 191(200:212) beads onto yarn before beginning (see page 116 for bead knitting tips).
With 2³⁄₄mm (No 12/US 2) needles, cast on 129(135:143) sts.
K 7 rows for garter st band.
Change to 3¹⁄₄mm (No 10/US 3) needles.
K one row.
P one row.
Beg bead patt border as foll:
1st patt row (RS) K1, *B1, k1; rep from * to end.
2nd patt row P to end.
3rd patt row K2, *B1, k1; rep from * to last 3 sts, B1, k2.
4th patt row P to end.
5th patt row K1, *B1, k1; rep from * to end.
This completes the bead patt border.
P one row.
Next row (dec row) (RS) K3, k2tog, k to last 5 sts, skpo, k3.
Cont in st st throughout, dec one st at each end of every foll 4th

row as set on **dec row** until 121(127:135) sts rem, and then every foll 8th row until 117(123:131) sts rem, so ending with a RS (dec) row.
Work 9(11:13) rows without shaping, so ending with a WS row.
Next row (inc row) (RS) K3, m1, k to last 3 sts, m1, k3.
Inc one st at each end of every foll 8th row as set on **inc row** until there are 129(135:143) sts, so ending with a RS (inc) row.
Work without shaping until back measures 31(32:33)cm/12¹⁄₄ (12¹⁄₂:13)in from cast-on edge, ending with a WS row.

Shape Armholes

Cast off 4(4:6) sts at beg of next 2 rows.
Work 2 rows without shaping, so ending with a WS row.
Next row (dec row) (RS) K4, sl 1, k2tog, psso, k to last 7 sts, k3tog tbl, k4.
Dec 2 sts at each end of every foll 4th row as set on last **dec row** until 109(111:115) sts rem, and then every foll 18th row until 101(103:107) sts rem.
Work without shaping until back measures 51(53:55)cm/20 (20³⁄₄:21³⁄₄)in from cast-on edge, ending with a WS row.

Shape Neck and Shoulders

Cast off 9(10:11) sts at beg of next 2 rows.
Divide for neck shaping on next row as foll:
Next row (RS) Cast off 9(9:10) sts, k until there are 12 sts on right-hand needle, then turn, leaving rem sts on a spare needle.
Working on this set of sts only for first side of neck, work one row without shaping.
Cast off rem 12 sts.
With RS facing, rejoin yarn to rem sts and cast off 41 sts for centre back neck, then k to end.
Complete to match first side.

LEFT FRONT

Thread 86(92:98) beads onto yarn.
With 2³⁄₄mm (No 12/US 2) needles, cast on 68(72:76) sts.
K 7 rows for garter st band.
Change to 3¹⁄₄mm (No 10/US 3) needles.
Next row K to last 10 sts, place these 10 sts on a st holder.
Next row Cast on one st at beg of row, then p to end. 59(63:67) sts.
Work 5 rows of bead patt border as for back.
P one row.
Next row (dec row) (RS) K3, k2tog, k to end.
Cont in st st throughout, dec one st at beg of every foll 4th row as set on **dec row** until 55(59:63) sts rem, and then on every foll 8th row until 53(57:61) sts rem, so ending with a RS (dec) row.
Work 9(11:13) rows without shaping, so ending with a WS row.
Next row (inc row) (RS) K3, m1, k to end.
Inc one st at beg of every foll 8th row as set on **inc row** until there are 59(63:67) sts, so ending with a RS (inc) row.
Work without shaping until front matches back to armhole shaping, ending with a WS row.

Shape Armhole

Cast off 4(4:6) sts at beg of next row.
Work 3 rows without shaping, so ending with a WS row.

Next row (dec row) (RS) K4, sl 1, k2tog, psso, k to end.
Dec 2 sts as set on last **dec row** on every foll 4th row until
49(51:53) sts rem, so ending with a RS row.
Work 17 rows without shaping, so ending with a WS row.
Next row (dec row) (RS) K4, sl 1, k2tog, psso, k end. 47(49:51) sts.

Shape Neck
Cast off 3 sts at beg of next row and 3 foll alt rows.
Dec one st at neck edge on next row and 2(3:3) foll alt rows.
Work 5(3:3) rows without shaping, so ending with a WS row.
Next row (dec row) (RS) K4, sl 1, k2tog, psso, k end. 30(31:33) sts.
Work without shaping until front matches back to shoulder
shaping, ending at armhole edge.

Shape Shoulder
Cast off 9(10:11) sts at beg of next row.
Work one row without shaping.
Cast off 9(9:10) sts at beg of next row.
Work one row without shaping.
Cast off rem 12 sts.

RIGHT FRONT
Thread 86(92:98) beads onto yarn.
With 2³/₄mm (No 12/US 2) needles, cast on 68(72:76) sts.
K 7 rows for garter st band.
Change to 3¹/₄mm (No 10/US 3) needles.
Next row K10 and place these sts on a st holder, k to end.
Next row P to end, then cast on one st at end of row. 59(63:67) sts.
Complete to match left front, reversing shapings by working 'skpo'
instead of 'k2tog', and 'k3tog tbl' instead of 'sl 1, k2tog psso'.

SLEEVES (make 2)
Thread 101(107:116) beads onto yarn.
With 2³/₄mm (No 12/US 2) needles, cast on 69(73:79) sts.
K 7 rows for garter st band.
Change to 3¹/₄mm (No 10/US 3) needles.
K one row.
P one row.
Work 5 rows of bead patt border as for back.
P one row.
Next row (inc row) (RS) K1, m1, k to last st, m1, k1.
Cont in st st throughout, inc one st at each end of every foll 8th
row as set on **inc row** until there are 91(95:103) sts.
Work without shaping until sleeve measures 29(30:31)cm/11¹/₂
(11³/₄:12¹/₄)in from cast-on edge, ending with a WS row.

Shape Sleeve Top
Cast off 4(4:6) sts at beg of next 2 rows.
Work 2 rows without shaping, so ending with a WS row.
Next row (dec row) (RS) K4, sl 1, k2tog, psso, k to last 7 sts,
k3tog tbl, k4.
Dec 2 sts at each end of every foll 4th row as set on **dec row** until
39 sts rem.
Work 3 rows without shaping, so ending with a WS row.
Next row (dec row) (RS) K4, k2tog, k to last 6 sts, k2tog tbl, k4.
P one row.

Dec one st at each end of next row as set on last **dec row**.
P one row.
Cast off 4 sts at beg of next 2 rows.
Cast off rem 27 sts.

LEFT FRONT BORDER (button band)
You will need to thread approximately 162(174:186) beads
onto yarn.
Using 2³/₄mm (No 12/US 2) needles and with RS facing, k across
10 sts on holder on left front.
Beg beaded border patt as foll:
1st row (WS) K5, p5.
2nd row [K1, B1] twice, k6.
3rd row K5, p5.
4th row K2, B1, k7.
Rep last 4 patt rows until band, when slightly stretched and ending
with a first patt row, fits up left front to neck edge.
Break off yarn but leave sts on a holder, then sew band in place.
Mark positions of buttons on button band, the first to be worked
on the 3rd row, the last in centre of neckband and the rem 5
spaced evenly between.

RIGHT FRONT BORDER (buttonhole band)
You will need to thread approximately 360(380:400) beads
onto yarn.
Using 2³/₄mm (No 12/US 2) needles and with WS facing, p5, k5
across 10 sts on holder on right front.
Beg beaded border patt as foll:
1st row (RS) K6, [B1, k1] twice.
2nd row P5, k5.
3rd row (first buttonhole row) K2, k2tog, yf, k3, B1, k2.
4th row P5, k5.
5th row (RS) K6, [B1, k1] twice.
6th row P5, k5.
7th row K7, B1, k2.
8th row P5, k5.
Rep 5th–8th patt rows until band, when slightly stretched and
ending with an 8th patt row, fits up right front to neck edge and **at
the same time** work buttonholes when reached as foll:
Buttonhole row (RS) K2, k2tog, yf, k1, work in patt to end.
Keep sts on needle and do not break off yarn, but sew band
in place.

NECKBAND
Using 2³/₄mm (No 12/US 2) needles and with RS facing, k6, [B1,
k1] twice across sts on right front band, pick up and k 26 sts up
left front neck, 11 sts down left back neck, 41 sts across back

*I used pewter-like beads to create a strong contrast against the
pastel background. You could use translucent crystal beads to
pick up the light and add sparkle to your knit.*

neck, 11 sts up right back neck and 26 sts down right front neck, then across sts of left front band [k1, B1] twice, k6. 135 sts.

Work buttonhole as for other buttonholes in centre of neckband when reached **and the at same time** cont beaded neckband patt as foll:

Next row (WS) K5, p4, p2tog, p to last 11 sts, p2tog, p4, k5. 133 sts.

Next row K7, *B1, k1; rep from * to last 8 sts, B1, k7.

Next row K5, p to last 5 sts, k5.

Next row K6, *B1, k1; rep from * to last 7 sts, B1, k6.

Next row K5, p to last 5 sts, k5.

K 8 rows. Cast off.

TO MAKE UP

Sew on sleeves, matching centre of sleeve to shoulder seam. Join side and sleeve seams. Sew on buttons.

Beaded Moccasins

Inspired by Native American footwear, these very special bootees are decorated by beads added with both the knit-in and sew-on techniques.

MATERIALS

1 x 50g (1³/₄oz) ball of Jaeger *Pure Cotton* in main colour (M) and a small amount in Dark Blue, Light Blue and Dark Red
Pair each of 2³/₄mm (UK No 12/US size 2) and 3¹/₄mm (UK No 10/US size 3) knitting needles
Small beads: 76 navy, 80 pale blue, 2 red and 30 white

SIZE

To fit 3–6 months

TENSION

25 sts and 34 rows to 10cm/4in over st st using 3¹/₄mm (UK No 10/US size 3) needles.

ABBREVIATIONS

B1 (bead 1) on RS rows = yarn to front of work, push bead up close to front of knitting, slip next st purlwise onto right-hand needle, then yarn to back of work leaving bead in front of slipped stitch.

B1 (bead 1) on WS rows = yarn to back of work, push bead up close to back of knitting, slip next st purlwise onto right-hand needle, then yarn to front of work leaving bead in back of slipped stitch.

See also page 21.

SPECIAL CHART NOTE

Read the chart from right to left on RS (odd-numbered) rows and from left to right on WS (even-numbered) rows. When working colour and bead patt from Chart A and colour motif from Chart B, use separate lengths of contrasting colour for each coloured area and twist yarns together on WS at joins to avoid holes.

TO MAKE

With 2³/₄mm (No 12/US 2) needles and yarn M, cast on 26 sts.
K one row.
Beg shaping sole as foll:
1 row K1, yf, k11, [yf, k1] twice, yf, k11, yf, k1.
2nd row K to end, working k1 tbl into each yf of previous row.
3rd row K2, yf, k11, yf, k2, yf, k3, yf, k11, yf, k2.
4th row As 2nd row.
5th row K3, yf, k11, [yf, k4] twice, yf, k11, yf, k3.
6th row As 2nd row.
7th row K4, yf, k11, yf, k5, yf, k6, yf, k11, yf, k4.
8th row As 2nd row.
9th row K5, yf, k11, [yf, k7] twice, yf, k11, yf, k5.
10th row As 2nd row. 51 sts.

Change to 3¹/₄mm (No 10/US 3) needles.
Cut Light Blue and Dark Blue yarns into 65cm/25¹/₂in lengths. Cut 6 Light Blue and 7 Dark Blue lengths. Thread 6 pale blue beads onto each length of Light Blue yarn. Thread 6 navy beads onto 5 lengths of Dark Blue yarn and 4 navy beads onto each of 2 rem lengths for edge sts.
Beg with a k row and working in st st, work 7 rows in colour and bead patt from Chart A, so ending with a RS row.
Change to 2³/₄mm (No 12/US 2) needles.
Using yarn M only, k 3 rows, so ending with a WS row.
Change to 3¹/₄mm (No 10/US 3) needles.

Shape Instep

Beg shaping instep as foll:
Next row (RS) K29, skpo, turn.
Next row Sl 1, p7, p2tog, turn.
Next row Sl 1, k7, skpo, turn.
Next row Sl 1, p7, p2tog, turn.
Beg Chart B colour motif in st st on next row as foll:
Next row Sl 1, k1, work across first row of Chart B, k1, skpo, turn.
Next row Sl 1, p1, work across 2nd row of Chart B, p1, p2tog, turn.
Rep last 2 rows 3 times more, but working 3rd–8th rows of Chart B.
Using yarn M only, cont as foll:
Next row Sl 1, k7, skpo, turn.
Next row Sl 1, p7, p2tog, turn.
Next row Sl 1, k7, skpo, k to end.
Next row P21, p2tog, p to end. 35 sts.
K 9 rows.
Next row K17, cast off one st, k to end.
Working on last set of 17 sts, k 20 rows for garter st cuff.
Cast off.
Rejoin yarn at centre to rem 17 sts and k 21 rows for garter st cuff.
Cast off. Work second moccasin in same way.

TO MAKE UP

Join sole and back seams. Using Dark Red yarn, embroider blanket stitch around outside edge of cuff and instep (see page 86 for how to work blanket stitch). Sew white, pale blue and red beads to instep as shown in photograph. Turn back cuff.

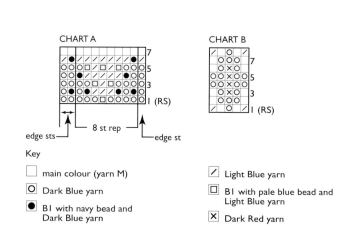

CHART A

7
5
3
1 (RS)

edge sts— ← 8 st rep → —edge st

CHART B

7
5
3
1 (RS)

Key

☐ main colour (yarn M)

◯ Dark Blue yarn

● B1 with navy bead and Dark Blue yarn

✓ Light Blue yarn

☐ B1 with pale blue bead and Light Blue yarn

✗ Dark Red yarn

YARN INFORMATION

Rowan and Jaeger Yarns

The following Rowan yarns and Jaeger yarns have been used for the knitting patterns in this book. See addresses below for obtaining these yarns. If you are purchasing a substitute yarn for the patterns, be sure to calculate the number of balls or hanks required by the number of metres (yards) per ball rather than by the yarn weight.

Rowan

Rowan *All Seasons Cotton*
a heavy-weight cotton yarn (60% cotton, 40% acrylic); approximately 90m (99yd) per 50g/1³/₄oz ball

Rowan *Cotton Glacé*
a lightweight cotton yarn (100% cotton); approximately 115m/125yd per 50g/1³/₄oz ball

Rowan *Denim*
a medium-weight cotton yarn (100% cotton); approximately 93m/101yd per 50g/1³/₄oz ball
Note: See page 11 for special care instructions for denim yarn, which shrinks in length after the first wash. Do not try to use a substitute for this yarn, as the pattern instructions are written specifically to compensate for the shrinkage.

Rowan *Magpie Aran*
an aran-weight wool yarn (100% pure new wool); approximately 140m/153yd per 100g/3¹/₂oz hank

Rowan *True 4-ply Botany*
a 4-ply yarn/US fingering weight (100% pure new wool); approximately 170m (186yd) per 50g/1³/₄oz ball

Jaeger

Jaeger *Cashmere*
a 4-ply yarn/US fingering weight (90% cashmere, 10% polyamide); approximately 98m/107yd per 25g/1oz ball

Jaeger *Baby Merino 4-ply*
a 4-ply yarn/US fingering weight (100% merino wool); approximately 183m/200yd per 50g/1³/₄oz ball

Jaeger *Matchmaker Merino Aran*
an aran-weight wool yarn (100% merino wool); approximately 82m/90yd per 50g/1³/₄oz ball

Jaeger *Pure Cotton*
a lightweight cotton yarn (100% mercerized cotton); approximately 112m/123yd per 50g/1³/₄oz ball

YARN STOCKISTS

Debbie Bliss's shop

Yarn, kits, ready-to-wear garments, books and toys are available from Debbie Bliss's shop:
Debbie Bliss
365 St John Street
London EC1V 4LB
Tel: 020 7833 8255
Fax: 020 7833 3588
Website:
www.debbiebliss.freeserve.co.uk

Rowan Yarns and Jaeger Yarns addresses

Rowan and Jaeger yarns are widely available in yarn shops. For details of stockists and mail order sources of the yarns, please write to or contact the distributors listed on this page and the next page.
For Rowan yarns, you can also visit their website:
www.rowanyarns.co.uk

Rowan Yarns

UNITED KINGDOM
HEAD OFFICE: RowanYarns, Green Lane Mill, Holmfirth, West Yorkshire HD7 1RW, England. Tel: (01484) 681 881.
Fax: (01484) 687 920.
Email: rowanmail@rowanyarns.co.uk

USA
DISTRIBUTOR: Rowan USA, 5 Northern Boulevard, Amherst, NH 03031.
Tel: (603) 886-5041/5043.
Email: wfibers@aol.com

AUSTRALIA
DISTRIBUTOR: Sunspun, 185 Canterbury Road, Canterbury, VIC 3126.
Tel : 03 9830 1609

BELGIUM
DISTRIBUTOR: Pavan, Koningin Astridlaan 78, B9000 Gent.
Tel: (09) 221 8594.

CANADA
DISTRIBUTORS:
Diamond Yarn, 9697 St Laurent, Montreal, Quebec H3L 2N1.
Tel: (514) 388-6188.
Diamond Yarn (Toronto), 155 Martin Ross, Unit 3, Toronto, Ontario M3J 2L9.
Tel (416) 736-6111.

DENMARK
STOCKISTS:
Aarhus: Ingers, Volden 19, 8000 Aarhus C. Tel : 86 19 40 44.
Kobenhavn: Sommerfuglen: Vandkunsten 3, 1467 Kobenhavn K.
Tel : 33 32 82 90.
Email: mail@sommerfuglen.dk
Nykobing: Ruzicka, St Kirkestraede 5 B, 4800 Nykobing F. Tel : 54 70 78 04.
Email: anne-lise@rudzicka.dk
Roskilde: Garnhoekeren, Karen Olsdatterstraede 9, 4000 Roskilde.
Tel: 46 37 20 63.

FRANCE
DISTRIBUTOR: Elle Tricot: 8 rue du Coq,
67000 Strasbourg.
Tel: 03 88 23 03 13.
Email: elletricote@agat.net

GERMANY
DISTRIBUTOR: Wolle & Design, Wolfshovener
Strasse 76, 52428 Julich-Stetternich.
Tel: 02461 54735.

HOLLAND
DISTRIBUTOR: de Afstap, Oude Leliestraat
12, 1015 AW Amsterdam.
Tel: 020-623 1445.

HONG KONG
DISTRIBUTOR: East Unity Co Ltd, Room 902,
Block A, Kailey Industrial Centre,
12 Fung Yip Street, Chai Wan.
Tel: (852) 2869 7110.

ICELAND
DISTRIBUTOR: Storkurinn, Kjorgardi,
Laugavegi 59, ICE–101 Reykjavik.
Tel: 551 8258.
Fax: 562 8252.
Email: stork@mmedia.is

JAPAN
DISTRIBUTOR: Diakeito Co Ltd, 2–3–11
Senba-Higashi, Minoh City, Osaka 562.
Tel: (0727) 27 6604.

NEW ZEALAND
STOCKISTS:
Auckland: Alterknitives, PO Box 30 645,
Auckland. Tel : (64) 937 60337.
Lower Hutt: John Q Goldingham, PO Box
45083, Epuni Railway, Lower Hutt.
Tel: (64) 4 567 4085.

NORWAY
DISTRIBUTOR: Ruzicka, Hans Aanrudsvei 48,
N-0956 Oslo. Tel: (47) 22 25 26 92.

SWEDEN
DISTRIBUTOR: Wincent, Norrtulsgaten 65,
11345 Stockholm. Tel: (08) 673 70 60.

Jaeger Yarns
UNITED KINGDOM
Jaeger Yarns, Green Lane Mill, Holmfirth,
West Yorkshire HD7 1RW, England.
Tel: (01484) 681 881.
Fax: (01484) 687 920.

USA
DISTRIBUTOR: Jaeger Yarns, 5 Northern
Boulevard, Amherst, NH 03031.
Tel: (603) 886-5041/5043.
Email: wfibers@aol.com

AUSTRALIA
DISTRIBUTOR: L & G Griffiths, PO Box 65,
Kilsyth, Victoria 3137. Tel: 03 972 86885.

BELGIUM
Distributor as Rowan.

CANADA
Distributors as Rowan.

FRANCE
Distributors as Rowan.

GERMANY
Distributors as Rowan.

HOLLAND
Distributors as Rowan.

HONG KONG
Distributors as Rowan.

ICELAND
Distributors as Rowan.

JAPAN
DISTRIBUTOR: Puppy Co Ltd, TOC Building,
7-22-17 Nishigotanda, Shinagawa-ku,
Tokyo. Tel: 03 3494 2395.

SWEDEN
Distributors as Rowan.

TAIWAN
DISTRIBUTOR: Green Leave Co Ltd, 6F1 No
21 Juen Kong Road, Chung Ho City,
Taipei Hsien. Tel: (886) 2 8221 2925.

Acknowledgements

This book would not have been possible without the invaluable contribution of the following people:

The knitters, Pat Church, Lynda Clarke, Penny Hill, Shirley Kennet, Maisie Lawrence, Beryl Salter and Frances Wallace.

Jane Bunce and Jane Crowfoot, whose help in the shop and contribution to ideas have been invaluable.

Penny Hill, for pattern compiling, and Marilyn Wilson, for her thorough checking.

Sally Harding, the editor, for her tremendous organisational skills.

Sandra Lane, for the beautiful photography.

Sammie Bell, for her lovely styling and contribution to the concept of the book.

Heather Jeeves, a fantastic agent.

Denise Bates, the commissioning editor, for being so supportive on all my Ebury projects.

Ciara Lunn, editorial assistant, for being simply wonderful.

Christine Wood, for her design concept of the book.

The models – a huge thank you to Max, Ceri, Cressy, Istvan, Ciara, Summer, Nell, Thea, Grace, Katie and Natalie.

Index

abbreviations, 21
Allen, Pam, 89
alpaca, 10
Aran designs: panels, 42
　throw, 51–3
　yarns, 44

baby knitting: cashmere scarf
　　and beanie hat, 28
　top with moss stitch trim,
　　32–3
backstitch, 25
bag, embroidered, 100
bead knitting, 116–18
　beaded cardigan, 120–3
　beaded moccasins, 124
beanie hat, 28
blanket, cashmere, 108
blanket stitch, 86
bobbles, 41
　bobble and lace edging,
　　104
　scalloped bobble edge, 104
　triangle bobble edging, 105
borders, textured knits, 44
buttons, 119

cable cast on, 15
cables: cable cushion, 50
　cabled sweater, 58–61
　panels, 42
　stitches, 40
　yarns, 44
cardigans: beaded cardigan,
　　120–3
　floral cardigan with picot
　　edge, 80–2
　girl's lace-edged cardigan,
　　110–13
cashmere, 10
　baby blanket, 108
cast-off edges, seams, 25
casting off, 19
casting on, 14–15
charts, colour knitting, 69
chevron lace, 105
children's knitting: child's
　　Guernsey with hood,
　　54–7
　child's smock, 90–3
　Fair Isle sweater, 76–9

V-neck tunic, 30
colour knitting, 68–72
　charts, 69
　child's Fair Isle sweater,
　　76–9
　colour swatches, 70
　combining colours, 71
　Fair Isle socks, 74
　floral cardigan with picot
　　edge, 80–2
　intarsia, 69, 72
　stranding, 68, 70
　weaving in, 68, 71
cords, knitting on double-
　　pointed needles, 116
cotton yarns, 10
cross stitch, 86
cushion, cable, 50

daisy edging, 104
decreases, 19
denim yarn, 10, 11
　embroidered denim jacket,
　　94–9
　man's denim Guernsey,
　　62–5
double moss stitch, 17
double-pointed needles,
　knitting cords, 116
duplicate stitch, 87

edgings, 104–7
　cashmere baby blanket,
　　107
　'framing' your knitwear, 106
　girl's lace-edged cardigan,
　　110–13
　inspirations, 107
　stitches, 104–5
embroidery, 86–9
　child's smock, 90–3
　denim jacket, 94–9
　embroidered bag, 100
　inspiration, 88–9
　stitches, 86–7
eyelet daisy edging, 104

faggoting with zigzag, 105
Fair Isle knitting, 71
　child's sweater, 76–9
　socks, 74
floral cardigan with picot
　　edge, 80–2
'framing' knitwear, 106

French knots, 86
funnel neck, raglan sweater
　　with, 34–7

garter stitch, 17
Guernseys: child's Guernsey
　　with hood, 54–7
　man's denim Guernsey,
　　62–5

hat, beanie, 28

increases, 18
intarsia knitting, 69, 72
jackets: embroidered denim
　　jacket, 94–9
　moss stitch jacket, 46–9

knit stitch, 16

lace: bobble and lace edging,
　　104
　chevron lace, 105
　girl's lace-edged cardigan,
　　110–13
　narrow lace edging, 104
linen yarn, 10

mattress stitch, 24
moccasins, beaded, 124
moss stitch, 17
　baby's top with moss stitch
　　trim, 32–3
　moss stitch jacket, 46–9

narrow lace edging, 104
needle conversion chart, 21

patterns, 20–1
picking up stitches, 25
picot edges, 105
　floral cardigan with picot
　　edge, 80–2
purl stitch, 16

raglan sweater with funnel
　　neck, 34–7
reverse stocking stitch, 17
ribbing: double, 17
　seams, 24

satin stitch, 87
scalloped bobble edge, 104
scarf, baby's cashmere, 28

seams, 24–5
selvedges, seams, 25
shaping, 18–19, 26–7
silk yarns, 10
slip knots, 14
small picot edge, 105
smock, child's, 90–3
socks, Fair Isle, 74
stem stitch, 86
stitches, 16–17
　cables, 40
　embroidery, 86–7
　sewing seams, 24–5
stocking stitch, 17
　knitting beads into, 116
stranding, 68, 70
swatches, colour, 70
sweaters: Aran sweaters, 42
　cabled sweater, 58–61
　child's Fair Isle sweater,
　　76–9
　child's Guernsey with hood,
　　54–7
　man's denim Guernsey,
　　62–5
　raglan sweater with funnel
　　neck, 34–7
　simple shapes, 26
Swiss darning, 87

tension, 20–1
terminology, 21
textured knits, 40–4
　Aran throw, 51–3
　cable cushion, 50
　cabled sweater, 58–61
　child's Guernsey with hood,
　　54–7
　man's denim Guernsey,
　　62–5
　moss stitch jacket, 46–9
throw, Aran, 51–3
thumb cast on, 14–15
triangle bobble edging, 105
tunic, child's V-neck, 30

washing, 11
weaving in, 68, 71
wool yarns, 10

yarns, 10, 126–7
　Aran textures, 44
　edgings, 107
　threading beads onto, 116